SMALL BUSINESS TAX HACKS

15 Essential Strategies to Minimize Liabilities, Maximize Deductibles, Increase ROI, and Unlock Financial Growth in Your Business

Tyler Harrison

Publisher

Copyright © 2024 Tyler Harrison

All rights reserved.

No portion of this book may be reproduced without written permission from the publisher or author except as permitted by U.S. copyright law. The content of this book may not be reproduced, duplicated, or transmitted without the author's or publisher's direct written permission.

Under no circumstances will any blame or legal responsibility be held against the publisher or author for any damages, reparation, or monetary loss due to the information contained within this book, either directly or indirectly.

Legal Notice:

This book is copyright-protected and is only for personal use. You cannot amend, distribute, sell, use, quote, or paraphrase any part of its content without the author's or publisher's consent.

Disclaimer Notice:

Please note that the information in this document is for educational purposes only. All efforts have been made to present accurate, up-to-date, reliable, and complete information. No warranties of any kind are declared or implied. Readers acknowledge that the author does not render legal, financial, medical, or professional advice. The content in this book has been derived from various sources. Please consult a licensed professional before attempting any techniques outlined in this book.

By reading this document, the reader agrees that the author is under no circumstances responsible for any direct or indirect losses incurred from using the information contained within it, including, but not limited to, errors, omissions, or inaccuracies.

CONTENTS

Title Page

Copyright

Introduction   1

Strategy 1-Master Tax Laws and Regulations   9

Strategy 2-Maximize Your Financial Advantage by Unlocking Deduction Secrets   24

Strategy 3-Business Structural Foundations as your Pillars of Prosperity   42

Strategy 4-Simplify your Bookkeeping to amplify business Brillance   56

Strategy 5-Master Payroll Perfection by Balancing Benefits and Burdens   71

Strategy 6-Expense Enlightenment is key to your deduction   96

Strategy 7-Capital Gains Mastery is a Path to Smart Investments   110

Strategy 8-Turn Time into Money by Dominating Depreciation   124

Strategy 9-Tax credit as a Financial Rewards   144

Strategy 10-Determine your Seasonal Strategy For filling your Tax   157

Strategy 11-Fortify Against Fiscal Audit Fears   173

Strategy 12-Guide Your Journey Through Changing Tax Laws	192
Strategy 13- Master Year-Round Tax Vigilance	209
Strategy 14-Answer to some Tax Mysteries	233
Strategy 15-Leap Over Tax Obstacles	260
Conclusion	276
Glossary	283
References	300

INTRODUCTION

Let's face it: taxes can be baffling, can't they? All that tax speak, those rules that change more often than we change our coffee filters—it's enough to make anyone's head spin. But guess what? You're not in this alone. Every small business owner has been there, scratching their head, trying to make sense of everything. That's where I come in.

I am a small business owner who transformed his tax turmoil into triumph. My experience and journey encapsulate the essence of resilience and adaptability. Like many, I was overwhelmed by the intricacies of tax regulations, viewing them as a daunting barrier to my business growth. However, through strategic learning and applying essential tax hacks, I turned my tax liabilities into opportunities for financial growth and business optimization.

Here is the thing: Imagine me as your friendly neighborhood tax guide, turning that bewildering tax talk into plain English so you can get back to doing what you love—running your business. So, please pull up a chair, take a deep breath, and let's tackle this tax thing together. After all, it's about making your business shine, and I'm here to help you polish it up—taxes and all.

This guide is inspired by my journey and countless other entrepreneurs who have successfully navigated the complexities of small business taxation. ***Small Business Tax Hacks: 15 Essential Strategies to Minimize Liabilities, Maximize Deductibles, Increase ROI, and Unlock Financial Growth in Your Business*** stands as a beacon, illuminating the path from confusion to clarity in managing tax liabilities.

This guide is not simply a collection of tax advice but a road map to transforming taxation from a daunting challenge into a strategic advantage for your business.

Confronting Tax Challenges Head-On

As a small business owner, you grapple with several tax-related challenges that can divert your focus from core business activities and growth. These challenges include navigating complex tax laws, maximizing deductions, choosing the proper business structure, maintaining effective recordkeeping, and minimizing tax liabilities.

That's exactly why I wrote this book. It's like your tax roadmap minus the confusing jargon. I'm sharing some smart moves and hacks I've learned to help you glide through the tax season, keep your books tidy, and even use the tax system to your advantage. You'll find practical examples, checklists, and templates that bring the strategies to life, enabling you to apply them directly to your business.

So, let's turn those tax lemons into lemonade and get you back to what matters—growing your dream. Ready?

Chapter Highlights-A Road Map To Tax Mastery

Here is a chapter-by-chapter preview of what is to come in your journey of business taxation discovery:

- **Understanding Tax Laws and Regulations:** Begin your journey with a solid foundation in tax laws affecting your business. Endeavor to learn how to navigate tax filing and payments and identify common mistakes to ensure compliance and avoid penalties.

- **Unlocking Tax Deductions:** Discover the power of intelligent deductions to reduce your tax bills significantly. This guide walks you through identifying eligible expenses and navigating changes in laws to maximize benefits.

- **Choosing Your Business Structure Wisely:** Your choice of business structure impacts taxes, liability, and funding. This book helps you weigh the pros and cons of structures like sole proprietorships, partnerships, LLCs, and S corporations to align with your goals.

- **Streamlining Bookkeeping:** Efficient bookkeeping is crucial for stress-free tax management. Adopt best practices, avoid common mistakes, and utilize tools to keep your financial records organized and accessible.

- **Navigating Payroll and Employee Benefits:** Manage payroll taxes and balance employee benefits effectively. Understand the distinctions between full-time and part-time employee taxes and ensure compliance.

- **Deciphering Business Expenses:** Understand what counts as a business expense. Track expenses accurately and understand their tax implications to leverage advantages fully.

- **Utilizing Strategies for Capital Gains:** Equip yourself with strategies to minimize capital gains tax and maximize depreciation benefits. Understand their calculations, claims, and impacts on your finances.

- **Making the Most of Depreciation:** Unlock the potential tax benefits for your small business by mastering the art of depreciation, from understanding its basics to navigating IRS rules and making strategic decisions.

- **Leveraging Tax Credits:** Investigate a range of tax credits, including the Work Opportunity Tax Credit and the Disabled Access Credit, that can significantly lower your business's tax burden.

- **Preparing for Tax Season:** A comprehensive checklist ensures you're well-prepared, from organizing financial records to consulting tax professionals for tailored advice.

- **Demystifying the Tax Audit Process:** Approach audits confidently by understanding the process, preparing effectively, and knowing how to respond, turning potential stress into a manageable task.

- **Staying Updated with Tax Law Changes:** In a landscape of evolving tax laws, remain informed and adaptable to leverage new opportunities and ensure compliance.

- **Planning for Taxes Year-Round:** Transform tax planning into a continuous activity that integrates seamlessly with your business operations, utilizing tools and strategies for ongoing optimization.

- **Tackling Common Tax Questions and Concerns:** Address your most pressing tax questions with practical solutions and insights, cutting through the clutter to provide clarity and confidence.

- **Overcoming Tax Hurdles:** The final chapter is dedicated to overcoming common tax concerns and objections, which provides the guidance needed to navigate tax challenges effectively.

Turning Knowledge Into Power

This guide provides small business owners with the necessary insights and resources to tackle the intricacies of taxation confidently. From understanding basic tax laws to leveraging deductions, choosing the proper legal structure, and mastering bookkeeping and payroll, you'll be better prepared to optimize your tax position, ensure compliance, and foster growth.

Additionally, it provides you with the necessary insights and resources to tackle the intricacies of taxation for small businesses confidently. By adopting a proactive approach to tax planning and embracing the strategies outlined, you can transform taxation from a source of stress into a strategic advantage.

Therefore, this is your invitation to turn the page and embark on the first step toward mastering the essentials of small business taxation and ensuring that the foundational elements directly empower your business. Through engaging storytelling, highlighting unique insights, and emphasizing practical application, *Small Business Tax Hacks* is not simply a guide but a companion in your entrepreneurial journey.

Let the transformation begin, from overwhelmed to overjoyed, as you unlock the secrets to your business's tax efficiency and financial growth.

STRATEGY 1-MASTER TAX LAWS AND REGULATIONS

"Knowledge is power, especially when it comes to taxes. The more you know, the less you owe.

Understanding Tax Laws and Regulations

As a small business owner, you're the backbone of the economy and a pioneer charting new territory. Dealing with tax laws and regulations can feel overwhelming, but it's crucial for your journey. In this chapter, you'll clearly understand basic tax laws, learn how to maximize deductions, and master the intricacies of tax filing and payments. You'll learn how to identify and sidestep common tax pitfalls. This is your guide to confidently manage your business taxes, empowering you to focus on what you do best—growing your business.

Basic Tax Laws and Regulations

As you navigate the evolving landscape of business taxation in 2024, staying informed about the latest tax laws and regulations is essential. Significant changes in corporate taxation, deductions, credits, and other areas will impact your business operations and financial strategies this year.

- **Corporate Tax Rate Changes:** In 2024, a significant change is on the horizon, with the proposed boost of the corporate income tax rate from 21% to 28%. This adjustment could substantially impact your business's financial outcomes, calling for reevaluating your fiscal strategies (*2024 Business Tax Laws*, n.d.).

- **Alterations in Deductions and Credits:** The new tax year brings changes aimed at promoting sustainable practices and growth. The Solar Investment Tax Credit (ITC) enhancement now allows for a 30% credit on solar projects that begin construction before 2025. More so, the Research and Development (R&D) Tax Credit has become more accessible, with eligible businesses now able to offset up to $250,000 of their payroll taxes, up from the previous $150,000. Additionally, adjustments in business loan interest deductions allow for up to 35% of adjusted taxable income, increased from the last 30% cap (*2024*

Business Tax Laws, n.d.).

- **Changes in Depreciation Rules:** New asset depreciation rules will impact your financial reporting and tax liabilities. For 2024, businesses can opt for a special bonus depreciation allowance of 60% for specific qualified property, down from 100% in 2022 and 80% in 2023 (*2024 Business Tax Laws*, n.d.).

- **Small Business-Specific Changes:** Small businesses will also see specific changes, such as increased standard deductions, revised mileage rates, and new employer tax credits for offering benefits such as paid family and medical leave, adoption assistance, or educational assistance.

- **Understand Tax Essentials:** Income tax pertains to the taxation of your business's income, determined annually according to its profits. Payroll tax encompasses the tax deducted from employee salaries to support social programs, while enterprises are responsible for collecting sales tax from customers on eligible sales transactions. Effective tax management is essential for maintaining your small business's financial well-being and adhering to regulations.

Adjusting to these changes is essential to ensure compliance and maximize economic advantages. Regular tax planning meetings, leveraging technology for compliance, and seeking specialist advice are vital for effectively handling these fresh regulations. Staying well-informed and taking proactive steps empower you to turn these challenges into opportunities for growth and success in the ever-changing realm of business taxation.

Tax Deductions for Small Businesses

Understanding tax deductions is crucial for small businesses to optimize financial health and ensure business prosperity. As a small business owner, you can lower your tax liability by taking advantage of various deductions, which are expenses subtracted from your income to determine your taxable income.

The top tax deductions include:

- **Business Meals:** You can deduct 50% of qualifying food and drink purchases related to your business (*25 Small Business Tax Deductions*, 2023).
- **Travel Expenses:** All work-related travel costs, including airfare, hotels, meals, and more, are deductible.
- **Home Office Expenses:** When you allocate a portion of your home for business purposes, you can claim deductions for expenses such as mortgage interest and utilities.
- **Office Supplies and Equipment:** Expenses for printers, paper, and computers used for business purposes are deductible.
- **Phone and Internet Expenses:** Based on your business usage, you can deduct a portion of your phone and internet expenses.

- **Business Insurance and Interest:** You can deduct business insurance costs and interest paid on business loans or credit cards.

- **Depreciation:** Spread out the expense of assets such as vehicles and equipment over their lifespan.

- **Professional Service Fees:** Legal, accounting, and other professional service fees necessary for your business are deductible.

- **Salaries and Employee Benefits:** If employees meet specific criteria, you can deduct their wages, benefits such as health insurance and retirement contributions, and vacation pay.

Additionally, understanding changes in tax laws and keeping precise financial records is critical for maximizing deductions. For instance, the Section 179 deduction allows small businesses to deduct the total cost of qualifying equipment in the year of purchase up to a specific limit (*Maximize Deductions: Smart Tax Strategies*, n.d.).

You can also discover deductions for contract labor, education expenses, inventory costs, business property rent, and software subscriptions. By deducting these expenses, you can effectively manage operational costs and reinvest in your business's growth.

Remember, each deduction has distinct prerequisites and limitations. So, it's advisable to consult a tax professional to tailor these strategies to your business's unique circumstances and comply with evolving tax regulations. By strategically leveraging available deductions, you can minimize tax liability and enhance your business's financial stability.

Tax Filing and Payments

Understanding and effectively managing tax filing and payments may seem challenging, but you can handle it smoothly with proper guidance. Start by determining your need to file a tax return, considering your income, tax filing status, age, and unique circumstances. Even if filing isn't mandatory, it could still be advantageous, particularly if you're eligible for specific tax credits such as the Child Tax Credit or Earned Income Tax Credit, which might result in a significant refund.

Remember, the tax filing deadline is April 15, 2024. If you cannot meet this deadline, ensure you file for an extension to push your due date to October 15, 2024. It's crucial to file your taxes by the deadline, even if you can't pay your tax bill, as avoiding filing can result in higher penalties (Parys & Orem, 2024).

Various free tax filing options are available for those with income below certain thresholds, such as the IRS Free File program and the Volunteer Income Tax Assistance (VITA) program. These services offer reliable assistance and ensure accurate returns. Additionally, if you expect a refund or need to settle your tax bill through your bank account, provide the correct routing and account numbers to your tax professional or software.

Maximizing your tax benefits involves understanding deductions and credits. Tax credits, such as the Child Tax Credit or American Opportunity Tax Credit, provide a dollar-for-dollar reduction in the tax owed, while deductions, such as those for charitable donations or medical expenses, reduce your taxable income.

Consider various tax filing options and tools, including online platforms, tax software solutions, and professional tax services. Online platforms offer convenience, while tax software balances user control and automated assistance. Professional tax services are ideal for complex tax situations or those seeking meticulous support.

Lastly, proactive, year-round tax planning is essential, especially for business owners or the self-employed who must make estimated tax payments. Staying informed about tax law changes, maximizing deductions and credits, and adjusting your withholding based on life changes are all part of effective tax management.

By staying organized, informed, and proactive, you can navigate the tax filing and payment process more smoothly, ensuring compliance and maximizing your returns.

Common Tax Mistakes and How to Prevent Them

Recognizing and avoiding common business tax mistakes ensures financial health and compliance. Here are fundamental points to help you navigate tax season successfully:

- **Classify Workers Correctly:** You may face significant legal and financial challenges if you misclassify employees as independent contractors. Hence, it's crucial to assess how much control you have over the worker and the duration of your relationship with them. Always refer to IRS policies and consider pursuing professional advice to avoid uncertainties.

- **Keep Proper Documents:** It's crucial to maintain accurate records. Common mistakes include not retaining receipts, mixing personal and business expenses, and overlooking mileage tracking. Implementing accounting software or employing a bookkeeper can help keep you organized and reduce errors.

- **Maximize Deductions and Credits:** Familiarize yourself with your company's tax credits and deductions. Standard deductions encompass costs such as rent, utilities, and employee wages. Credits range from incentives for hiring to investments in renewable energy, and it is essential to utilize these options to avoid overpaying taxes.

- **Pay Quarterly Estimated Taxes:** Paying taxes is an ongoing duty, not just a year-end obligation. Failing to pay quarterly estimated taxes can result in penalties and interest fees. Precisely determining your income and expenses, preferably with the guidance of a tax expert, is essential to avoid these challenges.

- **Address State and Local Tax Obligations:** Don't neglect state and local taxes. Each has unique laws and requirements. Non-compliance can lead to audits and legal troubles. Stay informed and work with professionals knowledgeable in these areas.

- **File and Pay Taxes Timely:** To avoid penalties and interest, stay organized and keep track of deadlines. Consider seeking professional help to guarantee you meet all filing and payment deadlines on time.

- **Separate Personal and Business Expenses:** Maintaining separate personal and business expenses is vital to avoid audits and ensures you get all deductions. By opening different accounts for your business, you can track costs accurately and claim all eligible deductions.

- **Seek Professional Help When Needed:** Tax laws present a complex landscape where failing to consult a tax professional can result in expensive errors and lost opportunities. Engaging a tax expert provides valuable insights and advice, guarantees adherence to regulations, and promotes your financial well-being.

Additionally, avoid other common errors such as choosing the wrong filing status, overlooking how life events affect taxes, and neglecting to include supporting documents with your tax return. Using the wrong tax form, failing to keep records throughout the year, and incorrectly entering information are also mistakes to be wary of.

With proactive steps and sound knowledge, you can confidently steer through tax season, ensuring accuracy and possibly realizing substantial savings.

Key Takeaways

- Stay informed about corporate tax rate changes, alterations in deductions and credits, and new depreciation rules in 2024 to maintain compliance and enhance financial strategies.

- Leverage tax deductions such as business meals, travel expenses, home office costs, and office supplies to lower tax liabilities and support business growth.

- Navigate tax filing and payments efficiently by understanding tax return requirements, meeting deadlines, and utilizing free tax filing options for eligible individuals.

- Recognize and avoid common tax mistakes such as misclassifying workers, maintaining accurate records, and maximizing deductions to ensure financial health and compliance.

- Stay organized, informed, and proactive in tax planning, ensuring timely compliance and maximizing potential tax benefits.

Having grasped the basics of tax laws, deductions, filing, and avoiding common mistakes, you're well-prepared to delve deeper. In the next chapter, we'll explore how to strategically maximize your tax benefits strategically, revealing opportunities to enhance your financial health and business growth.

STRATEGY 2-MAXIMIZE YOUR FINANCIAL ADVANTAGE BY UNLOCKING DEDUCTION SECRETS

"Every deduction is a step towards your business's financial freedom. Uncover them, claim them, thrive.

Unlocking Tax Deductions

Tax deductions are powerful tools often underestimated. As an entrepreneur, you must tap into the full potential of these commonly overlooked deductions, which are hidden gems that can significantly boost your financial health.

Whether you operate a sole proprietorship or a complex corporate structure, tailored deduction strategies await you. Stay agile as deduction laws evolve, ensuring your business remains at the forefront of tax efficiency. If doubts about deductions cloud your mind, let's dispel them together. Maximize your business's fiscal potential by digesting this chapter.

Unpacking the Power of Deductions

Every entrepreneur needs to understand the critical role of business tax deductions. You can significantly reduce your taxable income by strategically leveraging these deductions, leading to substantial savings. Here are some key points to consider:

- **Qualified Business Income Deduction:** Small businesses can deduct up to 20% of their income. For example, if your business earns $100,000, you can subtract $20,000 before taxes apply. However, high-income businesses can have limitations. As a lawyer, doctor, or consultant, if your income in 2024 exceeds $241,950 for single filers or $483,900 for married couples filing jointly, you'll begin to see a phase-out of your Qualified Business Income Deduction (Warshaw, 2024).

- **Home Office Deduction:** You can deduct expenses such as mortgage interest, insurance, utilities, and repairs if you exclusively use a part of your home for business purposes. The simplified method allows a deduction of $5 per square foot, up to 300 square feet (Warshaw, 2024).

- **Rent:** Renting a space for your business is fully deductible. This includes office spaces and retail locations.

- **Advertising and Marketing:** Expenses incurred in

promoting your business, such as social media ads and business cards, are deductible.

- **Office Supplies and Expenses:** Costs for everyday office supplies and larger purchases such as computers or smartphones used for business are also deductible.

- **Software Subscriptions:** Subscriptions required to operate your business, such as point-of-sale software, are deductible.

- **Vehicle-Related Deductions:** If your business operates vehicles, you can select the usual mileage rate or the actual expense method for deductions. This encompasses costs such as gas, upkeep, and insurance.

- **Professional Fees:** Fees for services such as accountants or financial advisors are often deductible as necessary business expenses.

Remember, while tax deductions can be highly beneficial, they should not drive your spending decisions. Deductions only lower your taxable income, not your costs. For instance, if you spend $1,000 on a business expense and are in a 22% tax bracket, your tax saving would be $220, not the total $1,000 (Watson, 2023).

Maintaining meticulous records and understanding each deduction category's nuances is essential. Consulting a tax professional offers personalized advice, ensuring maximized deductions and effective compliance with tax laws.

Tapping Into Commonly Overlooked Deductions

As a business owner, you must know the commonly overlooked tax deductions that can significantly reduce your taxable income. Here are some critical areas where you might find hidden savings:

- **Business Meals:** Deduct 50% of eligible meal expenses. This includes business meals during travel, which can be 100% deductible. Keep receipts and note the business purpose for each meal (Standberry, n.d.).

- **Hiring Your Children:** Employing your children can offer tax advantages. The payment made to them is deductible, and if it's less than the standard deduction, it can be tax-free for them.

- **Employee Salaries and Contract Labor:** Payments to employees and contractors are deductible. Ensure proper documentation such as W-4s for employees and W-9s for contractors.

- **Employee Benefit Programs:** Expenses for employee benefits, including health, educational assistance, FSAs, and retirement plans, are deductible. Some benefits also qualify for tax credits.

- **401(k) and Pension Contributions:** Contributions to retirement accounts such as SEP IRAs or Solo 401(k)s are deductible. For 2024, you can deduct up to $69,000 for such contributions (Standberry, n.d.).

- **Health Savings Account (HSA):** Contributions to an HSA are deductible, and funds used for qualified health expenses are not taxed.

- **Education and Training:** Deduct expenses for books, courses, seminars, workshops, and other materials related to your industry.

- **Equipment Rental and Insurance Premiums:** Deduct the total cost of rented business equipment and insurance premiums, including liability and property insurance.

- **Interest Paid on Loans:** You can claim deductions on interest from loans used for business activities, such as purchasing property or equipment.

- **Legal and Accounting Fees:** Deduct the costs of legal and accounting services you incur for your business.

- **Cell Phone and Home Internet Bills:** Deduct a portion of these bills based on the percentage used for business purposes.

- **Direct Home Office Expenses:** Expenses related directly to your home office, such as repairs and maintenance specific to the office area, are 100% deductible (Smiles, 2019).

- **Travel Expenses:** Deduct costs related to business travel, including airfare, car rentals, lodging, meals, and other incidentals.

- **Startup and Organization Costs:** Deduct costs associated with starting your business, such as licensing fees, permit fees, and professional fees.
- **Debt Interest and Loss Carryovers:** Deduct interest on business debts and carry over certain business losses to future tax years.
- **Inventory Costs:** Certain inventory costs, classified as materials and supplies, are deductible.
- **Bad Debts:** Write off bad debts such as unpaid accounts receivable or loans made through the business.
- **Parking and Tolls:** Keep receipts for parking and toll expenses related to business activities.
- **Local Travel Expenses:** Deduct costs for business-related local travel, such as Uber or taxi fares.

Remember, to claim these deductions legitimately, you must maintain detailed records and thoroughly understand IRS guidelines. It's advisable to seek advice from a tax professional to ensure compliance and fully leverage your tax savings.

Deductions for Different Business Structures

When selecting a business structure, understanding the tax implications is crucial. Here's a concise overview of different business structures and their tax considerations:

Sole Proprietorship

- **Taxation:** Income reported on the owner's tax return, taxed at individual rates.
- **Self-Employment Tax:** Owners pay Social Security and Medicare taxes on business income.
- **Personal Liability:** Business owners are responsible for their debts and obligations.

Partnership

- **Taxation:** Partners report income and losses on their tax returns.
- **Income Tax:** Taxed at individual partner's tax rate.
- **Self-Employment Tax:** General partners pay self-employment tax on their income share.
- **Liability:** Partners have shared liability, which can lead to personal financial risk.

Limited Liability Company (Llc)

- **Taxation:** An LLC can choose taxation as a corporation, sole proprietorship, or partnership.
- **Income Tax:** The business will benefit from pass-through taxation if treated as a sole proprietorship or partnership.
- **Self-Employment Tax:** Active members may be subject to this on their profit share.
- **Liability:** Offers limited liability protection to members.

Corporation

- **Taxation:** Corporations file a separate tax return.
- **Income Tax:** Dividends face taxation at the shareholder level, while corporate tax rates apply to the business.
- **Double Taxation:** Profits undergo taxation both at the corporate level and at the shareholder level for dividends.
- **Liability:** Offers strong protection against personal liability.

S Corporation

- **Taxation:** Profits and losses passed through to shareholders' tax returns.
- **Liability:** Offers protection of limited liability similar to that of a corporation.

Tax Planning Considerations

- **Deductions:** Different structures offer various tax deductions.

- **QBI Deduction:** Eligible pass-through entities and sole proprietorships can deduct up to 20% of qualified business income (*Tax Implications of Different Business Structures*, 2023).

- **Investment Income:** Business structures dictate different tax treatments.

- **Tax Credits vs. Deductions:** Credits directly reduce tax liability, while deductions lower taxable income.

The proper business structure is a pivotal choice affecting your tax obligations and compliance requirements. It's wise to seek guidance from a tax professional to understand how this decision impacts your business. Ensure the chosen structure matches your business objectives, risk appetite, and financial planning tactics.

Changes in Deduction Laws

Staying updated with changes in business tax deduction laws is crucial for several reasons:

- **Compliance:** Tax laws are constantly evolving, evidenced in 2024 by the increase in standard deductions for single and married filers, which affects how small business owners file their taxes. Not staying abreast of these changes can result in non-compliance, potentially leading to penalties and legal issues.

- **Financial Planning:** Understanding recent updates, such as the revised mileage rates for business-related transportation expenses, is vital for accurate economic forecasting and budgeting. This knowledge lets you plan your costs more effectively and maximize potential savings.

- **Maximizing Deductions:** Changes in tax laws often include modifications to deduction limits and the introduction of new credits. For example, the IRS updated tax credits related to energy efficiency, such as the Residential Clean Energy Credit, and introduced employer tax credits for benefits, such as paid family and medical leave. Being informed means maximizing these deductions and reducing your overall tax burden.

- **Strategic Decision Making:** Tax law changes can influence business decisions. For instance, lowering the e-filing threshold to 10 returns and updating energy efficiency tax credits can impact how you manage your accounting processes and investments in sustainable resources (*2024 Tax Law Changes*, n.d.).

- **Avoiding Surprises:** Tax laws, such as the resumption of student loan payments and their implications on tax filings, can unexpectedly impact your financial obligations. Staying updated helps anticipate these changes and prepare accordingly.

Monitoring deduction law updates on business tax is crucial to ensure compliance, strategically plan finances, maximize deductions, make knowledgeable business decisions, and prevent unforeseen financial challenges.

How to Overcome Concerns About Deductions

As a business owner, navigating the landscape of tax deductions can be challenging, but optimizing your tax strategy is essential. Here are practical steps to effectively manage your business tax deductions:

- **Understand What's Deductible:** First, familiarize yourself with the various deductions available to your business. Standard deductions include startup costs, inventory, utilities, insurance, rent for business property, vehicle expenses, depreciation, home office deductions, advertising and marketing expenses, office supplies, software subscriptions, legal and professional fees, and interest on business debts.

- **Keep Meticulous Records:** Detailed recordkeeping is crucial. Ensure you document all your business-related expenses. This can include maintaining logs for vehicle use, keeping receipts for office supplies, and recording utility bills if you claim a home office deduction.

- **Use the Right Accounting Tools:** Leveraging accounting software can help you track expenses accurately and facilitate tax filing. These tools can also offer insights into possible tax savings.

- **Consult a Tax Professional:** Tax laws are often intricate and change-prone. Therefore, it's essential to collaborate with a CPA or a tax advisor.

- **Understand the Specifics of Each Deduction:** Every deduction comes with specific criteria. For instance, you must use a part of your home exclusively and regularly for business to qualify for the home office deduction. Additionally, you can deduct vehicle expenses using the standard mileage rate or calculating the actual costs. Understanding these details is essential to maximize your deductions legally.

- **Consider Depreciation and Section 179 Deductions:** For business assets such as equipment and vehicles, understand depreciation rules and the Section 179 deduction. Having full knowledge of these two can provide substantial tax savings over time.

- **Plan for Major Purchases and Investments:** If you plan to make significant investments in equipment or other capital expenses, consider the timing. Aligning these purchases with your tax strategy can optimize deductions.

- **Stay Informed About Changes in Tax Laws:** Tax regulations undergo continuous changes, and it's essential to remain vigilant and well-informed about any updates that might impact your business deductions.

By combining knowledge, meticulous recordkeeping, and professional advice, you can effectively manage your business tax deductions, potentially reducing your tax liability and enhancing your business's financial health.

Key Takeaways

- Unlock significant savings by wisely utilizing deductions such as the Qualified Business Income and Home Office Deduction.

- Fully deduct rent for business spaces and all advertising, marketing, and office expenses.

- Choose between standard mileage or actual expense methods for vehicle-related deductions and deduct professional service fees.

- Don't let deductions drive spending; remember, they reduce taxable income, not expenses.

- Explore commonly overlooked deductions, including business meals, hiring your children, and various employee benefits.

- Maximize your deductions with accurate record-keeping and an understanding of IRS guidelines.

- Choose the proper business structure (sole proprietorship, partnership, LLC, corporation, S corporation) for tax efficiency.

- Stay informed about changes in deduction laws for compliance, financial planning, and maximizing deductions.

- Effectively manage tax deductions by understanding what's deductible, maintaining meticulous records, using accounting tools, and consulting tax professionals.

- Leverage depreciation and Section 179 deductions for business assets, and stay updated on evolving tax laws.

Delving deeper into the nuances of tax deductions and aligning these insights with the best business structure to maximize tax benefits is crucial. In the next chapter, we'll help you choose a framework that effectively complements your tax strategy.

STRATEGY 3-BUSINESS STRUCTURAL FOUNDATIONS AS YOUR PILLARS OF PROSPERITY

"Your business structure is the chassis on which your financial success rides. Choose wisely.

Choosing Your Business Structure Wisely

Business structure is everything when it comes to taxation. It's a pivotal crossroads that would shape the future of your venture; hence, it is required that you choose wisely. This chapter will guide you through the legal complexity of business structures. Whether you resonate with the independent spirit of a sole proprietorship, value the unity in a partnership, seek the balance of an LLC, or aim for the elevation of an S corporation, you can navigate all of these with clarity and insight.

Each structure offers unique benefits and challenges tailored to different visions and goals. Understand the nuances, weigh your options, and when doubt lingers, remember consulting a professional can turn uncertainty into your strategic advantage. Let's embark on this journey together to help you make informed choices that secure your business's foundation and propel its growth.

Sole Proprietorship: The Lone Ranger's Guide

Embracing a sole proprietorship could be key to having an uncomplicated and autonomous entrepreneurial journey. This business structure epitomizes simplicity, directly linking your personal and business identities. As a sole proprietor, you're the captain of your ship, who is faced with making all decisions and steering the course of your venture.

This approach seamlessly integrates your business and personal finances, with your business income flowing directly to you. For example, as a freelance graphic designer, the income from your projects is your income, and you're responsible for all tax obligations.

The appeal of a sole proprietorship stems from its straightforward setup and minimal regulatory requirements. You bypass the complexities of filing separate business tax returns and overseeing corporate governance. However, this simplicity also means you assume full responsibility for any debts or legal challenges your business encounters, potentially putting personal assets such as your home or savings at risk in legal disputes.

Yet, for many entrepreneurs, particularly small business owners, consultants, and freelancers, the allure of total control and flexibility outweighs these risks. The success of your sole proprietorship hinges on your skills and business savvy, making it a favored choice for those who value straightforward management and personal autonomy in their business endeavors.

Partnership: The Power of Collaboration

In a partnership, you're not just pooling resources but creating a powerful synergy by combining unique skills, expertise, and connections. Picture yourself in a dynamic team where members contribute to shared goals with distinct abilities.

Imagine a tech start-up and a seasoned marketing firm teaming up: the start-up brings innovative technology, while the marketing firm offers deep knowledge and a broad network. This union enables achievements far beyond what they can accomplish individually.

Effective communication—characterized by openness, honesty, and adaptability—is crucial in partnerships. It's about understanding each other and making decisions that benefit all parties. Embrace partnerships to unlock new opportunities, perspectives, and growth.

This collaborative journey isn't only about individual success but about working together toward mutual goals and catalyzing extraordinary achievements in business, community projects, or personal ventures. Remember, in the world of partnerships, when you collaborate effectively, everyone wins.

Limited Liability Company (LLC): The Middle Ground

As an entrepreneur, when you form a limited liability company (LLC), you access a potent mix of advantages: the asset protection found in a corporation coupled with the flexibility and tax benefits typical of a partnership.

By choosing an LLC, you shield your assets, such as your home, car, and savings, from legal troubles or debts incurred by your business. Creditors typically can't touch your assets even if your LLC faces legal challenges.

From a tax perspective, you can select your business's tax classification as either a sole proprietorship, partnership, or corporation, which can result in significant tax savings. Pass-through taxation, a common choice for small businesses, allows your profits and losses to directly impact your tax return, allowing you to bypass the double taxation typical in corporations.

LLCs also offer operational freedom with fewer requirements for recordkeeping and meetings, allowing you to focus more on growing your business. This structure is ideal for solo entrepreneurs and team-based ventures, offering a balanced approach to protecting and enhancing your business.

S Corporation: The Next Level

As an S corporation owner, you stand to gain significant tax advantages while enjoying the legal protections typical of a standard corporation. Unlike C corporations, S corporations allow you to transfer profits and losses directly to your tax returns, avoiding the higher corporate tax rates. This means you could enjoy significant tax savings, particularly in a lower tax bracket.

For example, with an annual S corp income of $100,000, you report this directly on your tax return, potentially benefiting from a lower rate than corporate taxes.

However, remember that S corps have strict eligibility criteria, including being a domestic corporation with certain types of shareholders, a cap of 100 shareholders, and only one class of stock. Therefore, you must adhere to corporate formalities such as forming a board of directors and holding regular meetings.

Choosing an S corp ensures personal asset protection against business liabilities and avoids the double taxation traditional corporations face. It's crucial to meet all these requirements to fully leverage an S corporation's tax benefits and liability protection.

C Corporation: The Right Choice for Your Small Business?

Opting for a C corporation structure offers your small business the potential for immense growth and robust asset protection. Like large corporations, you can raise capital through stock sales, offering a clear path to scale your business. This structure also acts as a protective barrier, safeguarding your assets from business-related debts and legal issues.

However, this path comes with significant challenges, including double taxation. In this scenario, the government taxes your company's profits at the corporate level and then taxes the dividends distributed to shareholders, including you, at the personal level. This can notably affect your financial position compared to LLCs or S corps structures.

Additionally, be prepared for a heavier administrative load involving more complex paperwork, adherence to regulations, and potentially higher costs for legal and accounting services. If you're ready to navigate these challenges and embrace the opportunities that come with a C corporation, these could be key to elevating your business to new heights.

Legal Structure Factors to Consider

Selecting the proper business structure is essential for your success. Each kind offers specific benefits and drawbacks, so weighing these factors is necessary:

- **Liability:** Think about how much personal liability you're willing to assume. In sole proprietorships and partnerships, your assets are vulnerable to legal challenges against your business. Conversely, corporations and limited liability companies (LLCs) protect your assets, shielding them from business debts and legal judgments.

- **Taxation:** Your business's tax obligations heavily depend on its structure. In sole proprietorships, partnerships, and LLCs, "pass-through" taxation applies, where the business income undergoes taxation just once on your tax return. Conversely, corporations experience "double taxation," where the government taxes profits at both the corporate level and then as shareholder dividends.

- **Funding:** If you plan to raise capital, consider a structure that appeals to investors. Corporations, especially C corporations, are often preferred for raising venture capital or going public. In contrast, sole proprietorships may need help attracting significant external funding.

- **Control and Management:** Sole proprietorships offer complete control but demand significant personal commitment. Partnerships share this burden but require aligned vision and trust. Corporations and LLCs provide a more formal structure, potentially reducing emotional strain but also diluting your control.

- **Flexibility and Future Needs:** Think long-term. A sole proprietorship might be sufficient now, but a corporation or LLC may offer more benefits and opportunities as your business grows.

- **Costs and Paperwork:** Consider each structure's costs and regulatory requirements. A sole proprietorship is the easiest to form, whereas a corporation requires more paperwork and has ongoing regulatory requirements.

For example, consider a freelance graphic designer opting for a sole proprietorship for simplicity and complete control. However, if they plan to scale up, forming an LLC might better protect personal assets and offer more credibility.

Your choice shapes your business journey, so weigh these factors in light of your goals, resources, and risk tolerance. Remember, the proper structure aligns with your business strategy, offering a foundation for growth and success.

When to Consult a Professional

Deciding on a proper structure when you launch a business is crucial. You may ask yourself, "Do I need professional help with this decision?" The response is a resounding *yes*, particularly in specific scenarios.

First, evaluate your business's complexity. You might manage the decision independently for a simple solo venture, such as freelance writing. However, seeking professional guidance is crucial for more intricate endeavors involving partnerships, significant investments, or cutting-edge technology. A business advisor can clarify the distinctions among sole proprietorship, partnership, LLC, and corporation, customizing their recommendations to fit your specific scenario.

Imagine you're launching a tech start-up with the potential for rapid growth and significant liability. A professional can analyze these factors and suggest a structure, such as an LLC or corporation, that protects liability and accommodates future expansion.

Moreover, tax implications play a crucial role. Different structures have varied tax responsibilities and benefits. A tax professional will help you understand these complexities, ensuring you choose a structure that optimizes your tax position.

Finally, a lawyer's expertise is invaluable if your business involves legal agreements or intellectual property. They'll ensure that your business structure safeguards your assets and interests. A business attorney helps choose the best legal structure that minimizes tax liabilities and suits your business model.

Engaging a professional is wise when your business is intricate, exposed to considerable liabilities, or dealing with complex tax and legal issues. Their expertise will give you peace of mind and a solid foundation for the business's success.

Key Takeaways

- A sole proprietorship is ideal for individuals seeking simplicity and direct control, but it comes with the risk of personal liability for business debts.

- Partnerships thrive on collaboration and shared skills but require effective communication and mutual respect among partners.

- Limited liability companies (LLCs) offer asset protection and tax flexibility, making them suitable for those seeking corporate benefits without extensive formalities.

- S corporations provide tax advantages and protect personal assets but come with strict eligibility requirements and more rigorous corporate formalities.

- C corporations allow for significant growth through stock sales and offer limited liability but face double taxation and increased regulatory demands.

- Choosing the proper business structure requires considering liability, taxation, funding, control, flexibility, future needs, and administrative costs.

- Consulting a professional is crucial for complex businesses, significant tax implications, or legal intricacies to ensure the optimal structure for your business needs.

Now that you've explored the legal landscapes for your small business, we will turn our focus to efficient bookkeeping. Mastering this crucial skill ensures financial health and compliance, laying a solid foundation for your business's success and longevity. The next chapter unveils these critical insights.

STRATEGY 4-SIMPLIFY YOUR BOOKKEEPING TO AMPLIFY BUSINESS BRILLANCE

"Efficient bookkeeping isn't just about numbers; it's about narrating your business's success story and transforming complex numbers into clear, actionable insights.

.Streamlining Bookkeeping

Imagine the peace of mind you'll gain by building a robust bookkeeping foundation, ensuring every financial step you take is on solid ground. Tax season becomes a stress-free experience with the right system, not a dreaded chore.

Embrace the best practices of recordkeeping; they're your shield against the anxiety of audits. Avoid common pitfalls that trap many business owners, ensuring your path is clear and unobstructed. Embrace cutting-edge tools and apps that transform bookkeeping from a tedious task to an empowering business strategy. This is your guide to turning bookkeeping from a liability into a powerful asset.

Building a Solid Bookkeeping Foundation

As a small business owner in the United States, establishing a robust bookkeeping system is critical for your success. Small businesses, which make up $33.2 million of the U.S. economy and have created 12.9 million new jobs from 1996 to 2021, face the challenge of a high failure rate, with 20% failing in their first year (Sehmbi & Kriss, 2023). This underscores the importance of strong financial management for your company's longevity and success.

Effective bookkeeping entails accurately recording and organizing financial transactions, a vital step in meeting legal and tax obligations. Proper bookkeeping can protect your business from penalties, fines, and legal disputes, safeguard your reputation, and support smooth business growth. It empowers you to make strategic decisions by providing insights into your business's strengths, weaknesses, and opportunities.

For instance, as a start-up owner, analyzing profitability helps you focus on the most lucrative services or products, significantly impacting your business's growth and long-term success.

Financial credibility, demonstrated through meticulous bookkeeping, is crucial for securing funding and building strong investor relationships. Since 54% of small business owners start with personal funds, showcasing financial stability through solid bookkeeping is essential (*2023 Small Business Statistics*, 2023).

Despite the importance, about 70% of small businesses operate without an accountant, and 60% of owners lack sufficient accounting knowledge, creating compliance issues and barriers to understanding their business's financial health (Martinez, 2023).

Adopting the latest technology in accounting, such as cloud-based software used by 95% of accounting practices, is beneficial. This technology has been shown to improve client services and increase profits, with the accounting market projected to grow to $1,009.51 billion by 2026 (Martinez, 2023).

As a small business owner, investing in effective bookkeeping practices and technology is not just fulfilling a regulatory requirement; it's a strategic investment in your business's future.

Choosing the Right Bookkeeping System

A suitable bookkeeping system is pivotal for your small business's financial soundness and expansion. Identify your needs: Do you require a system for multiple users or businesses? Would a cloud-based solution or mobile app enhance your operations?

Explore reputable accounting software options such as QuickBooks, known for its comprehensive features and automation; FreshBooks, ideal for contractors or small businesses; Sage 50cloud, which integrates with Microsoft 365; or Wave Accounting, an accessible and user-friendly choice. Each software offers distinctive attributes to suit diverse business requirements.

Understanding the basics of bookkeeping is crucial. You must actively engage in data entry, transaction categorization, accounts receivable management, and payroll administration. Even with automated software, a solid grasp of these processes ensures effective financial oversight.

Choose between single-entry and double-entry accounting systems based on your business size and needs. For simpler operations, a single-entry system might suffice. However, a double-entry system offers a more detailed financial picture, capturing equity, assets, and liabilities.

Decide on an accounting method:

- Cash-basis: Recording transactions when cash changes hands
- Accrual-basis: Recording invoices and bills upon issuance or receipt for a comprehensive financial view

Evaluate your bookkeeping management options: DIY, hire a part-time bookkeeper, use a SaaS solution, delegate to an employee, or outsource. Consider each method's pros and cons about your business scale and needs.

Avoid mistakes like mixing personal and business finances, disorganized records, or inadequate expense tracking. Regularly reconcile financial records and secure data back-ups.

Lastly, don't hesitate to seek expert help when needed. Services such as Bench or Bookkeeper.com can provide invaluable assistance, ensuring organized, compliant, and strategically planned financial management. Your choice in bookkeeping should align with your business's needs and resources, setting a solid foundation for economic management and business growth.

Recordkeeping Best Practices

Practical financial control is vital for the success of an entrepreneur. Here's how you can ace it:

- **Embrace Digital Solutions:** Shift to digital records. This move enhances accessibility and efficiency in bookkeeping and tax preparation while minimizing risks linked to paper records.

- **Implement a Document Management System:** Adopt a digital recordkeeping system to organize your finances better.

- **Understand Record Retention Requirements:** Keep business records, especially those related to income, deductions, and credits, for at least seven years to comply with tax regulations.

- **Choose the Right Software:** Opt for accounting and payroll software that simplifies creating records such as invoices and tax forms and streamlines your bookkeeping.

- **Regular Reconciliation:** Make it a habit to reconcile bank statements with your records to identify and correct discrepancies and ensure accuracy.

- **Back-Up Your Data:** Always have a backup of your digital records, preferably in cloud-based storage.

- **Separate Personal and Business Finances:** Keep different accounts for personal and company use to simplify tax filing and auditing.

- **Track Every Transaction:** Record every transaction meticulously, regardless of size, to maintain precise financial records.

- **Leverage Accounting Software:** Utilize software for recording transactions, managing receipts, and reconciling accounts.

- **Know Recordkeeping Durations:** Remember the duration for which you should retain different records, per IRS guidelines.

- **Maintain Organized Financial Management:** Keep detailed records of all financial aspects, including sales, expenses, payroll, and taxes.

- **Facilitate Tax Compliance:** Accurate recordkeeping is essential for correct income, expense, and deduction reporting during tax seasons.

- **Make Informed Decisions:** Use comprehensive records to make critical business decisions about expansion, investments, or hiring.

- **Showcase Business Viability:** Well-maintained records

demonstrate your business's stability and management, which are essential for funding or loans.

- **Stay Regulation Savvy:** Keep abreast of legal changes to ensure regulatory compliance.

- **Monitor Receivables and Payables:** Maintain precise invoices and cash flow records.

- **Plan for Growth:** Use your financial history to strategize for future needs and opportunities.

- **Minimize Fraud and Errors:** Regular reconciliation and internal controls help reduce fraud and mistakes.

By adhering to these recordkeeping practices, you comply with regulations and gain a powerful tool to understand and steer your business toward success. Remember, robust financial management is the backbone of a thriving business.

Common Bookkeeping Mistakes to Avoid

Avoiding common bookkeeping mistakes is crucial for small business success. Here are critical mistakes to avoid:

- **Hire Skilled Professionals:** Engage skilled bookkeepers and accountants to ensure precise financial records and compliance with regulatory standards, a critical step in focusing on your business growth.

- **Maintain Proper Records**: To facilitate easy tax filing and audit processes, keep accurate records of all financial transactions and receipts, preferably in electronic formats.

- **Separate Personal and Business Finances:** Establish distinct bank accounts for personal and business use to streamline cash flow management and simplify audits.

- **Categorize Income and Expenses Accurately:** Properly classifying income and expenses is essential for correct profit reporting and avoiding tax issues.

- **Track All Receipts and Expenses:** Document every receipt, even minor ones, and track reimbursable expenses to maintain accurate records and maximize tax deductions.

- **Reconcile Bank Statements Regularly:** Align your

bookkeeping records with bank statements to ensure accuracy and promptly identify discrepancies.

- **Stay Informed on Sales Tax:** Understand and follow sales tax laws to avoid fines and fines.

- **Review Financial Statements:** Regularly examine your balance sheet and income statement for insights into your business's financial health.

- **Manage Petty Cash Effectively:** Implement a robust system for petty cash, including logging all expenditures and appointing a responsible custodian.

- **Classify Employees Correctly:** Distinguish between employees and contractors to avoid tax penalties and legal issues.

- **Implement Internal Controls:** Establish solid internal measures to prevent fraud and theft, significant petty cash, and employee expenses.

- **Back-Up Financial Records:** Regularly protect your financial data against loss by backing it up.

By embracing these strategies, you not only prevent common bookkeeping mistakes but also lay a solid foundation for your company's financial soundness and expansion.

Bookkeeping Tools and Apps

As a small business owner, you'll find it essential to have highly effective bookkeeping tools at your disposal to help manage your finances efficiently. Let's highlight some of the most outstanding bookkeeping tools and applications that have proven invaluable for small businesses over the years:

- **QuickBooks Online:** This comprehensive tool offers secure invoicing, advanced reporting, multi-user access, and mileage tracking. Its standout features include 1099 contractor filing and extensive reporting capabilities. While not the cheapest option, its wide array of attributes justifies the investment.

- **Wave:** Perfect for freelancers and small businesses, Wave is a standout free accounting and invoicing software. It allows unlimited users and invoicing and provides a robust chart of accounts. Its accounting and invoicing services are free, with only nominal fees for payment processing.

- **Sage Business Cloud Accounting:** Aimed at start-ups and small-scale businesses, Sage offers a cloud-based, flexible, and scalable accounting solution, making it an ideal choice for those who need adaptable accounting tools.

- **Bill.com:** Excellent for automating accounts payable and receivable, Bill.com seamlessly integrates with popular accounting software such as QuickBooks, Xero, Sage, and Oracle. This integration simplifies managing invoices and payments, enhancing efficiency in your financial processes.

- **Expensify:** A top choice for expense report management, Expensify streamlines the process of capturing receipts and tracking expenses, which is crucial for maintaining accurate financial records in small businesses.

- **Finagraph:** This tool provides crucial insights into your business's financial health, aiding in strategic growth and budgeting planning, ensuring you make informed financial decisions.

- **Hubdoc:** Ideal for document management, Hubdoc automates the collection and organization of financial documents, easing the maintenance of organized and accessible financial records.

- **Cloud-Based Accounting Software:** Options such as FreshBooks or Xero can automate transaction recording, invoice generation, and more, offering a comprehensive solution for financial management.

- **Receipt Tracking Apps:** Apps such as Receipt Bank or Shoeboxed digitize and categorize receipts, streamlining the expense tracking process.

- **Expense Tracking Apps:** Tools such as Expensify or Zoho Expense help keep track of all business expenses, ensuring thorough financial oversight.

- **Virtual Bookkeeping Services:** Services such as Bench or Bookkeeper.com offer professional bookkeeping expertise at a cost-effective rate, providing the benefits of experienced bookkeepers without the high expense.

When choosing the right bookkeeping tool for your business, ensure it aligns with your needs. The ideal tool will significantly improve financial management, freeing time and resources for other critical business areas. Engaging actively with the best-suited tool fosters smoother and more efficient business operations.

Key Takeaways

- Establish a solid bookkeeping foundation, which is vital for your small business and impacts legal compliance and decision-making.

- Choose the right bookkeeping system by understanding your business needs, selecting suitable software, and determining the best accounting methods and entry systems.

- Implement effective recordkeeping by going paperless, using document management systems, following record retention rules, and consistently reconciling and backing up records.

- To strengthen your business's financial foundation, engage professional expertise, maintain meticulous records, separate personal and business finances, and regularly review your financial statements.

You're perfectly equipped to handle payroll and employee benefits as you've mastered the bookkeeping essentials. This critical step is essential for ensuring compliance and boosting employee satisfaction, which secures your business's financial well-being. Let's explore these critical aspects together, breaking down complexities and strengthening your monetary strategy.

STRATEGY 5-MASTER PAYROLL PERFECTION BY BALANCING BENEFITS AND BURDENS

"Great businesses are built on great teams. Manage payroll and benefits like a pro, and watch your team — and business— flourish.

Payroll and Employee Benefits

You're at the heart of your business's success, and mastering payroll taxes and employee benefits is crucial for your journey. This chapter is your compass through the complex world of payroll taxes, transforming deductions from daunting to manageable. In this chapter, we'll balance the scales between employee benefits and tax obligations, ensuring you understand their impact on your business's financial health.

Whether dealing with full-time or part-time staff, you'll gain insights into the tax implications and compliance strategies. This chapter aims to empower you to optimize costs and maximize the value of your employee benefits. Let's navigate these challenges together, ensuring your business thrives.

Understanding Payroll Taxes

As a small business owner, you must grasp payroll taxes for compliance and your business's financial well-being. Here's a clear, concise guide to help you understand this intricate subject:

- **Types of Payroll Taxes:** Payroll taxes consist of federal income tax, Social Security and Medicare taxes, Additional Medicare Tax, Federal Unemployment Tax (FUTA), Self-Employment Tax, and a range of state and local taxes.

- **Federal Income Tax:** Withhold federal income tax from employees' wages using the details on their W-4 forms.

- **Social Security and Medicare Taxes:** In 2024, workers and employers contribute to Social Security and Medicare taxes. Employees contribute 6.2% of their paychecks to Social Security and 1.45% to Medicare, and their employers match these contributions (*Payroll Taxes for Small Businesses*, 2023).

- **Additional Medicare Tax:** This applies to employees earning over $200,000 annually, at a rate of 0.9%, without an employer match (*Payroll Taxes for Small Businesses*, 2023).

- **FUTA:** This is paid by employers at 6% on the first $7,000 paid to each employee annually (*Payroll Taxes for Small Businesses*, 2023).

- **Self-Employment Tax:** This involves self-employed individuals, encompassing employer and worker contributions to Social Security and Medicare taxes.

- **State and Local Taxes:** These taxes vary, depending on your business location, and may include additional payroll taxes for state disability, workers' compensation, and unemployment tax funds.

- **Payroll Tax Compliance:** It is vital to fit and report your payroll taxes accurately to avoid penalties. Use Forms 941, 943, 944, 945, and 940 for reporting, and consider using payroll services for compliance and accuracy (*Payroll Taxes for Small Businesses*, 2023).

- **Calculating Payroll Taxes:** Calculate taxes based on employees' total wages and deductions, including federal and state income taxes, FICA, and potentially local taxes. The payroll tax rate, including employer and employee contributions, generally totals around 15.3% (7.65% each for employer and employee). This includes both parties' 6.2% for Social Security and 1.45% for Medicare (*Payroll Taxes for Small Businesses*, 2023). Accurate computation and payment of FICA taxes are mandatory. Failure to do so can lead to penalties. It's vital for smooth financial management and legal compliance.

- **Employer Responsibilities:** As an employer, you must accurately withhold the right amounts for taxes and pay your portion of FICA and FUTA taxes. For self-employed individuals, you are responsible for covering both the employer's and employee's parts of payroll taxes.

Remember that while payroll taxes significantly impact your business expenses, they are vital in funding essential social programs such as Medicare, Social Security, and unemployment benefits. By complying with legal requirements, your business not only meets legal standards but also enhances the welfare of your employees and contributes positively to the community.

Employee Benefits and Tax Obligations

Managing employee benefits and handling tax obligations are critical tasks for a small business owner. Here's a detailed guide to navigating these complex areas effectively:

Employee Benefits: The Incentives

Offering employee benefits goes way beyond mere gestures. It's an investment in your company's future. Consider it akin to sowing seeds that will blossom into a dedicated and driven workforce. Small business owners often favor retirement plans such as SEP-IRAs, 401(k)s, and SIMPLE 401(k)s. These plans not only cater to the future needs of employees but also provide immediate financial advantages through tax-deductible contributions.

When considering paid employee leave, it's important to note that offering paid leave for medical and personal reasons can qualify you for a tax credit. This credit usually varies between 12.5% and 25% of the employee's leave amount (Fallon, 2023).

Tuition reimbursement is a smart move, too. It not only fosters employee growth but also is a tax-deductible perk. You can reimburse your employees for a part or all of their tuition, with the benefit being tax-deductible up to $5,250 per employee per year (Fallon, 2023).

Tax Obligations: The Responsibilities

Managing taxes is an indispensable element of any business operation. Handling payroll taxes efficiently and contributing to Medicare and Social Security programs is crucial. Remember that you and your employees share the responsibility for these taxes. Additionally, be mindful of certain limitations, such as the wage base limit for Social Security.

The Federal Unemployment Tax Act (FUTA) and State Unemployment Tax Act (SUTA) are also on your plate. FUTA is an employer-only tax, while SUTA varies by state, and timely payments can qualify you for a federal tax credit.

Employee Tax Withholding And Reporting

Your tax responsibilities include withholding employee taxes, depositing them, reporting on them, and making payments. Be diligent in using forms such as Form W-4 for employee withholding, Form 941 for filing quarterly tax returns, and Form W-2 for providing wage and tax statements.

As a small business owner, understanding the importance and function of IRS Form W-4, the Employee's Withholding Certificate, is crucial for effective payroll management. This form is critical for calculating the accurate federal income tax and FICA tax employers must deduct from their employees' paychecks. Here are some key points to consider:

- **Employee Information Gathering:** Form W-4 collects essential information about your employees, such as their marital status and any additional deductions they might qualify for. This information directly influences the tax you must withhold from their paychecks. For example, two employees earn the same salary, but one is single and lives in Boston, Massachusetts. The other is married with three children and resides in Omaha, Nebraska. The employer will withhold more tax from the paycheck of the single employee in Boston than the married employee in Omaha.

- **Compliance With Tax Regulations:** By accurately filling out and utilizing the information from Form W-4, you ensure compliance with tax withholding regulations, thus avoiding potential penalties and legal issues.

- **New Hire Reporting:** Form W-4 reports new hires to relevant tax authorities. Collecting a W-4 form from each new employee when they start working at your business is a legal requirement.

- **Adaptation to Employee Life Changes:** Employees should update their W-4 forms whenever they experience significant life changes (such as marriage, having a child, etc.) that could affect their tax situations. Staying current with these changes helps you withhold the correct amount of tax.

- **Employee Assistance:** It's beneficial to assist your employees in understanding and completing the W-4 correctly. This includes providing resources or guidance on filling out the form, especially for those unfamiliar with it. Remember, while you can guide them, you should refrain from giving direct advice on how to fill specific sections.

- **Integration With Payroll Systems:** Utilizing digital tools for processing W-4 forms can greatly enhance accuracy and efficiency. These tools help automate collection, storage, and management, ensuring accurate tax withholdings and compliance with regulations.

By adequately managing Form W-4, you comply with legal requirements and ensure the financial well-being of your business and employees. Accurate withholding prevents situations where employees might face unexpected tax bills or receive large refunds, promoting better financial planning and employee satisfaction.

Strike a balance between offering competitive benefits and fulfilling your tax obligations. Benefits such as retirement plans, paid leave, and tuition reimbursement attract quality employees and provide tax advantages.

Full-Time vs. Part-Time Employees

As a small business owner, you must grasp the tax consequences of employing part-time versus full-time workers. Both types of employment carry distinct tax responsibilities and benefits, which can significantly impact your business's financial health.

Full-Time Employees

- **Payroll Taxes:** Whether an employee works full-time or part-time, you must withhold payroll taxes from their paycheck. This comprises local, state, and federal income taxes and Social Security, Medicare, unemployment, and disability insurance, if applicable.

- **Federal Insurance Contributions Act (FICA):** Both employers and workers are responsible for equally contributing to the withholdings for Social Security and Medicare.

- **Unemployment Taxes (FUTA):** You must pay these if you pay at least $1,500 to an employee each quarter and have at least one employee for 20 weeks each year. It is currently equal to 6% of the employee's applicable wages. (Lasker, 2022).

- **Health Insurance:** The Affordable Care Act mandates that businesses with 50 or more full-time employees provide health insurance. Conversely, smaller businesses with less than 50 full-time workers can offer optional health insurance. If they do, they gain a competitive advantage, even though it's not mandatory (Wiebe, 2023).

Part-Time Employees

- **Flexibility in Payroll:** Part-time employees often work variable hours, leading to fluctuating payroll expenses. While you still need to withhold taxes as with full-time employees, part-time staff might not be eligible for certain benefits, reducing overall costs.

- **Benefits Consideration:** Part-time workers typically receive limited retirement plans and health insurance benefits. This strategy can result in considerable cost savings for your business.

- **Impact on Tax Credits:** Employing part-timers can affect your eligibility for certain small business tax credits, especially those related to healthcare and retirement benefits.

Key Considerations

- **Classification:** Be careful when classifying employees. Typing a full-time employee as part-time can result in legal and financial penalties.

- **Compliance:** Adhere to the Fair Labor Standards Act (FLSA) and ACA. These laws have different criteria for defining full-time and part-time employees and dictate corresponding responsibilities.

- **Healthcare Law Requirements**: Under the ACA, your workforce's classification as full-time or part-time can define you as a small employer or an applicable large employer, each with different obligations.

Remember, each type of employment has its unique tax implications. Understanding these differences is vital to make informed hiring decisions and maintain financial and legal compliance. Consulting with a tax professional or accountant is highly advisable to navigate these complex aspects.

Steps to Stay Compliant on Payroll Taxes

Navigating payroll taxes as a small business owner might seem daunting, but you can manage it effectively and avoid penalties by following the proper steps. Here's how you can stay compliant with payroll tax requirements:

- **Identify Taxable Workers:** Determine which workers are subject to payroll taxes. Most employees fall under this category, but exceptions, such as independent contractors, exist. Misclassifying workers can lead to penalties.

- **Determine Taxable Wages:** Calculate taxable wages for each employee, including regular wages, salaries, and bonuses. Remember, pre-tax deductions such as retirement plan contributions affect taxable wages.

- **Calculate and Withhold Taxes Accurately:** Use reliable payroll software or a service provider to correctly calculate withholdings for federal income tax, Social Security, Medicare, and any state or local taxes. Incorrect calculations can lead to penalties.

- **File and Remit Taxes on Time:** Timely filing and remittance of payroll taxes are crucial. Use forms such as 941 or 944 for federal taxes and appropriate state forms. Late submissions can incur penalties (*Payroll Tax*

Compliance, n.d.).

- **File W-2s Annually:** You must file W-2 forms for each employee by January 31 of each year, reporting taxable wages and withholdings (Asmussen, 2023).

- **Know Updated Tax Laws:** Tax statutes frequently change. Stay informed through reputable sources, workshops, or consulting with a tax professional.

- **Understand Local and State Compliance:** Stay informed about the payroll tax requirements specific to your state or locality. These prerequisites encompass withholding taxes and unemployment taxes. Remember, each state sets its own rules and has different reporting obligations.

- **Maintain Accurate Records:** Maintain thorough records of salaries, deductions for taxes, and the submission of payroll taxes. It would be best if you did this to ensure precise reporting and prepare for potential inquiries from tax authorities.

- **Respond to Government Correspondence Promptly:** If you receive letters from the IRS, SSA, or state authorities, address them immediately to avoid missing important deadlines.

- **Consider Professional Assistance:** If payroll tax compliance seems overwhelming, consider hiring a certified public accountant or using a payroll service. They can enhance precision and adherence to regulations, streamline processes, and avoid expensive errors.

To manage your payroll taxes effectively, follow these steps to ensure your business complies with regulations and avoids unnecessary penalties. Staying informed and taking necessary actions is essential to manage payroll taxes successfully.

Employee Benefits: Balancing Cost and Value

As an entrepreneur, understanding the complexities of balancing cost and value and the worker's benefits is crucial. Offering comprehensive and attractive employee benefits, especially health insurance, is essential for the well-being of your employees and their families and for retaining talent in your company.

These benefits can attract and retain the best talent but also have tax implications. Health insurance premiums paid by you are tax-deductible, reducing your taxable income. Employees also benefit as their pre-tax dollars fund their contributions, which reduces their taxable income. Retirement plans such as 401ks or SEP IRAs offer tax-deductible contributions for employers.

Flexible Spending Accounts (FSAs) and Health Savings Accounts (HSAs) allow for pre-tax contributions, offering payroll tax savings for employers. Other benefits, such as dependent care assistance and commuter benefits, also provide tax efficiencies. It's vital to report and document these benefits correctly for compliance. Seek professional guidance to navigate these tax implications effectively.

Employee benefits also have financial implications. Thus, it's vital to understand them.

- **Cost and Contribution:** The primary expense in group health insurance is the premium typically shared between you and your employees. Factors such as workforce size, employee demographics, and the chosen insurance plan influence costs. For example, the age-banded rates in small business group health plans mean premiums can vary significantly based on employees' ages. For small businesses, most insurance premiums are tax-deductible as they are considered a necessary cost of doing business. This includes premiums for workers' compensation, general liability, credit insurance, group hospitalization and health insurance for employees, malpractice insurance, commercial property insurance, business overhead insurance, commercial auto insurance, and business interruption insurance. However, exceptions include certain life insurance or annuity premiums and policies covering earnings lost due to sickness or disability. It would be best if you kept abreast of the annual changes in IRS guidelines.
- **Cost and Coverage:** The plan design and coverage options you select also impact costs. More comprehensive coverage comes with a higher price tag, so it's crucial to balance robust coverage for effective cost management.

Consider plans with higher deductibles and maximum out-of-pocket costs to lower monthly premiums. For example, suppose you own a tech start-up in Silicon Valley and provide health insurance to your employees. In that case, these contributions are typically not subject to federal income and FICA taxes. This not only offers tax-free benefits to your employees for the premiums you cover but also allows you to deduct these expenses from your business taxes.

- **Employee Utilization and Preventive Care:** How employees use healthcare services can significantly affect insurance costs. Higher claims and medical expenses lead to increased premiums upon renewal. Educating employees on healthcare utilization, promoting wellness programs, and offering preventive care options are vital strategies to manage these costs.

- **Administrative Costs:** When considering offering group health insurance, it's crucial to account for the administrative costs involved. These include managing enrollment, processing claims, and ensuring compliance with regulations. These factors are critical in evaluating the decision to provide group health insurance.

- **Regulatory Compliance:** Understand the compliance

requirements, such as COBRA for employers with 20 or more employees and Section 125 reporting for offering pre-tax benefits (Bryant, 2023).

As a small business owner, you must understand the importance of implementing the Consolidated Omnibus Budget Reconciliation Act (COBRA) in your business practices. COBRA is a federal law enacted in 1985 that allows employees and their families to continue health insurance coverage under the employer's plan in certain instances where coverage would otherwise be lost, such as termination of employment or reduction in work hours (Leonard, 2023).

Here's how COBRA can be relevant and beneficial to you:

- **Eligibility and Requirements:** If your business has 20 or more full-time employees and offers health insurance, you must typically provide COBRA coverage. This also applies to part-time employees whose combined hours meet this threshold. Many states have similar laws for businesses with fewer than 20 employees, often called "mini-COBRA" plans (Leonard, 2023).

- **Employee Coverage:** COBRA permits individuals and their dependents to continue their health coverage in case of job termination (unless due to gross misconduct), reduced work hours, divorce, or the employee's death.

However, they are responsible for paying the entire premium cost themselves.

- **Duration of Coverage:** Depending on the qualifying event, COBRA coverage typically lasts for 18 to 36 months (Leonard, 2023). To accurately determine the duration of coverage, it is essential to understand the unique aspects of each case thoroughly.

- **Employer Responsibilities:** You are responsible for notifying employees and their spouses about their COBRA rights and health coverage at the start of their employment. You must also provide a COBRA qualifying event notice in the event of a qualifying event.

- **Cost and Administration:** While COBRA can be more expensive for individuals than regular health plans (as they must pay the total premium cost, including the part previously covered by the employer), it does not typically require extra costs from the employer, aside from a possible 2% administrative charge (Leonard, 2023).

- **Non-Compliance Risks:** Failure to comply with COBRA can lead to significant penalties. These include fines imposed by the Department of Labor and potential legal action from employees or beneficiaries denied their COBRA rights.

- **Recordkeeping and Notices:** Accurate recordkeeping

and timely provision of notices are crucial for COBRA compliance. Consider using HR software or outsourcing benefits administration to manage these responsibilities effectively.

- **Decision Period for Coverage:** Employees have 60 days after a qualifying event to decide whether to opt for COBRA coverage (Leonard, 2023).

Understanding and effectively managing COBRA requirements can ensure legal compliance, benefit your employees during transition times, and avoid hefty fines and legal complications.

When designing your employee benefits package, prioritize aligning benefits with what employees expect while balancing cost-effectiveness and value. To achieve this, utilize regular surveys and feedback mechanisms to tailor benefits to the diverse needs of your employees. Small businesses can also consider unconventional benefits such as flexible scheduling, employee assistance programs, or telecommuting to enhance value without incurring substantial expenses.

Additionally, creating a total compensation summary for each employee can help them understand the actual value of the benefits offered. If you're updating your benefits package, develop a communication plan to ensure employees understand the changes and the impact of new benefits.

Lastly, technology solutions should be considered to integrate benefits administration with payroll processing, reducing administrative burden and potential errors while staying compliant with regulations.

Key Takeaways

- Understand payroll taxes, including federal income tax, Social Security, Medicare, and FUTA, and learn accurate withholding and reporting methods.

- Offer employee benefits such as retirement plans, paid leave, and tuition reimbursement, balancing costs with tax-deductible advantages.

- To remain payroll tax compliant, follow the steps to identify taxable workers, calculate taxable wages, withhold taxes accurately, file and remit taxes on time, and maintain accurate records.

- Balance the cost and value of employee benefits, especially health insurance, by understanding premiums, plan design, employee utilization, and regulatory compliance.

- Stay informed and proactive about changes to tax laws and regulations, and consider professional assistance for complex payroll and benefits management.

- Utilize technology solutions to integrate benefits administration with payroll processing to reduce administrative burden.

Let's focus on understanding and breaking down business expenses after navigating the intricacies of payroll taxes and employee benefits. This next chapter will empower you with the knowledge to manage your business expenses effectively, ensuring your financial health and compliance.

STRATEGY 6-EXPENSE ENLIGHTENMENT IS KEY TO YOUR DEDUCTION

"Every expense tells a story. Understand it, and you unlock insights into your business's soul.

Deciphering Business Expenses

Steering your enterprise through the ever-shifting seas of financial management is not easy. However, having the know-how of categorizing business expenses is not just necessary; it's your power tool for clarity and control. Imagine transforming the mundane task of tracking expenses into your strategic advantage, enabling you to craft reports that speak volumes.

When it comes to taxes, understanding the impact of each expense transcends mere compliance—it's about making informed decisions that bolster your business's financial health. Embrace this journey to master your business finances, fortifying your venture's foundation for enduring success.

Categorizing Business Expenses

Correct categorization of business expenses is crucial for your financial success. It enables precise budgeting, tax optimization, and strategic decision-making, ensuring a strong financial foundation for your business. Understanding what counts as a deductible expense and what doesn't is essential. Here are some key categories and tips:

- **Vehicle Use:** These costs are deductible if you use your vehicle for business or have a car strictly for business. This includes the standard mileage rate or actual expenses, if well-documented.

- **Travel Expenses:** Remember, you can deduct costs such as airfare, lodging, and meals when traveling for business, as long as the primary purpose of the trip is for business.

- **Equipment:** Deduct office furniture, computer hardware, and other essential business technology expenses. The deductibility, however, hinges on the equipment's type and specific use in your business operations.

- **Insurance:** Premiums for business liability insurance, property insurance, or workers' compensation are deductible. The rules for deducting insurance expenses vary, so consult a tax professional.

- **Advertising and Marketing:** Costs for promoting your business, including digital and print campaigns, are usually deductible. These expenses help acquire and retain customers.

- **Professional Services:** Ensure that the fees you pay for legal, accounting, or consulting services, often deductible, are ordinary and necessary for your business's industry.

- **Education and Training:** You can deduct costs associated with business-related courses or seminars, provided they are directly relevant to your business or necessary for maintaining your professional skills.

- **Supplies and Office Expenses:** Day-to-day office supplies and operational costs, such as website hosting and software, are deductible.

- **Utilities and Telephone Costs:** These include keeping your business operable, such as electricity, water, and phone bills. For home offices, only the portion used for business is deductible.

- **Non-Deductible Expenses:** Certain expenses, such as lobbying costs, political donations, personal commuting, and illegal activities, are not deductible. Entertainment expenses and business gifts exceeding $25 per person also fall into this category (*How to Categorize Your Business Expenses*, 2023).

To manage your business expenses efficiently, maintain a separate bank account and credit card. This simplifies tracking and categorizing expenses. Keep digital copies of receipts and use software or tools for expense tracking. Regularly categorizing and reviewing your expenses helps in accurate tax filing and can save you from unnecessary tax liabilities.

Tracking Business Expenses

Effective tracking of business expenses is a critical aspect of financial management that can significantly enhance a company's reporting and overall financial health. Here's a comprehensive list of why and how to track business expenses:

Importance Of Tracking Business Expenses

- **Budget Creation and Management:** Tracking expenses enables a business to create a realistic budget, forecast future spending, and manage funds efficiently. This proactive approach helps avoid cash flow slowdowns and ensures critical expenses, such as payroll, are always met.

- **Tax Deductions and Compliance:** Tracking expenses accurately is essential, ensuring they are both "ordinary and necessary" for your business. You must also categorize and document costs meticulously, which is critical to complying with tax regulations and avoiding potential audit complications.

- **Cash Flow Optimization:** Regularly monitoring expenses helps maintain sufficient cash reserves and make informed decisions about using credit lines or loans. This is essential for managing short-term financial gaps and planning long-term financial strategies.

- **Cost Savings Identification:** Businesses can spot unnecessary costs and adjust by analyzing expenses. Regular expense analysis is also crucial to benchmarking against industry standards and identifying areas for cost reduction.

Strategies For Effective Expense Tracking

- **Open a Separate Business Bank Account:** This step involves separating business and personal finances, simplifying the bookkeeping process, and increasing transparency.

- **Choose the Right Accounting Software:** You can automate and streamline the expense tracking process using QuickBooks, NetSuite, or Sage Intacct. Seek out features such as expense categorization, vendor management, and the ability to integrate with other business tools when considering these platforms.

- **Use Dedicated Business Credit and Debit Cards:** These cards help organize expenses and offer additional benefits such as credit history access and rewards programs. They also streamline transaction recording.

- **Maintain Accurate Records and Receipts:** Keep detailed records of all expenses and receipts. Digital tools often allow for the electronic storage of invoices, which is essential for tax purposes and audits.

- **Review and Categorization of Expenses Regularly:** Periodic analysis of expenses helps identify trends and areas for cost reduction. Categorizing expenses aids in better financial planning and tax preparation.

- **Train Employees and Implement Policies:** Regular training on expense tracking procedures ensures compliance and accuracy. Establish a clear expense policy to guide the recording and approval processes.

Benefits Of Accurate Expense Tracking

- **Improved Budget Forecasting:** Accurate expense tracking leads to more effective budget allocation and reduces the risk of fund shortfalls.

- **Reliable Financial Reporting:** Accurate expense recording is crucial for financial statements. This transparency is vital for investor confidence and regulatory compliance.

- **Tax Management:** Correctly categorizing and recording expenses are essential for practical tax computation and compliance.

Tracking business expenses is essential for regulatory compliance, financial growth, and stability. By adopting the appropriate methods and tools, you can seamlessly integrate this process into the success framework of your business.

Understanding the Tax Implications of Your Business Expenses

Grasping the tax implications of your business expenses is critical to enhancing your financial well-being and staying in line with tax regulations. Let's dive into a thorough guide to steer you through this essential aspect:

- **Tax Deductions and Credits:** Most businesses can claim deductions on various expenses, reducing their taxable income. Examples include rent, utilities, advertising, and employee salaries. However, certain costs, such as start-up and organizational costs, are considered capital expenses and amortized over several years (McIntyre, 2021). Tax credits directly reduce your tax liability, matching each dollar saved with a dollar less owed. Notable instances of these credits encompass research and development incentives, employee retention benefits, and small business healthcare deductions.

- **Sales and Payroll Taxes:** Sales tax on specific products and services differs from state to state. As a business owner, you must comply with your state's tax regulations. Additionally, payroll taxes encompass deductions for Social Security, Medicare, federal and state income taxes, and unemployment taxes. Accurately classifying your workforce as either employees or independent contractors is pivotal. This determination directly impacts your payroll tax responsibilities.

- **International Operations:** You must understand double taxation agreements and foreign tax credits if your business operates internationally. Digital sales, especially, have specific tax implications.

- **Tax Filing Deadlines and Audits:** Be aware of different tax filing deadlines based on your business structure. Accurate records are essential for tax filing and supporting your returns in case of an IRS audit.

- **Recordkeeping:** Accurate and detailed record keeping is critical. This includes maintaining receipts, invoices, and other documentation for deductible expenses. Remember, depending on their use, some costs are only partially deductible.

- **Different Types of Expenses:** Operating expenses encompass daily expenditures such as salaries and utility bills, while capital expenses pertain to durable assets such as equipment that serve long-term purposes. On the other hand, non-operating expenses are unrelated to a business's fundamental operations, such as the interest incurred on loans.

- **Tax Professionals:** Given the intricate nature of tax regulations and their varying effects on businesses of different types, seeking advice from a tax expert is recommended. They can provide valuable insights into deductions and credits and ensure adherence to tax laws.

Remember, effective management of your business expenses and understanding their tax implications is not just about minimizing your tax liability; it's also about ensuring legal compliance and optimizing the financial health of your business.

Key Takeaways

- Categorizing expenses correctly and distinguishing between deductible and non-deductible costs is vital for financial success.

- Deductible expenses include vehicle use, travel, equipment, insurance, advertising, professional services, education, supplies, and utilities.

- Non-deductible expenses cover lobbying, political donations, personal commuting, and illegal activities.

- Practical strategies for expense tracking include using dedicated business accounts, choosing suitable accounting software, and maintaining accurate records.

- Understanding tax implications involves knowing about deductions, credits, sales and payroll taxes, and international operations.

- It is wise to seek guidance from a tax expert when dealing with intricate tax regulations and optimizing tax tactics.

Having explored the nuances of categorizing, tracking, and understanding the tax implications of your business expenses, you're now well-prepared to delve into capital gains. The next chapter will empower you with strategies to maximize tax efficiency and bolster your business's financial health.

STRATEGY 7-CAPITAL GAINS MASTERY IS A PATH TO SMART INVESTMENTS

"In the world of business, the wise are those who turn capital gains into capital growth.

Utilizing Strategies for Capital Gains

You're standing at a crucial juncture in your business's path, where grasping the nuances of capital gains can significantly shape your financial triumph. Every transaction and every asset sale holds growth potential. Yet, it's crucial to grasp the fundamentals of capital gains tax to safeguard your hard-earned profits.

Don't worry—you're not on your own. Effective strategies can reduce your taxes and increase your savings. This guide empowers you to make informed decisions, turning tax challenges into opportunities to sustain and expand your business dream.

Capital Gains as a Primer for Small Businesses

Selling a capital asset, such as a business, real estate, or stocks, at a price higher than its initial purchase price leads to capital gains. This profit represents the disparity between the selling and buying prices. For example, if your Oregon-based Software Company acquires a software program for $2,000 and sells it for $5,000, you earn a capital gain of $3,000.

You may not be required to pay capital gains tax when you sell certain assets. For instance, the sale of inventory is capital gains exempt. If your Texas car shop sells a car for profit, you don't report it as capital gain but as business income.

There are two categories for capital gains: realized and unrealized. Realized gains occur when you sell an asset, while unrealized gains are theoretical, representing an increase in value that has no cash conversion yet. Understanding the impact of realized and unrealized capital gains is crucial as a small business owner. Realized gains from selling assets for more than their purchase price increase your taxable income, affecting your tax liability. Unrealized gains, increases in the value of assets you still own, only impact your taxes once sold.

How Do Capital Gains Benefit Small Businesses?

- **Investment Opportunities:** Small businesses frequently need capital for growth, technological investments, or operational expansion. Capital gains emerge as a critical funding source when you sell assets or business shares. You can use these gains to reinvest in your business, facilitating growth, enabling new hires, or initiating new product launches.

- **Tax Advantages:** Capital gains often come with tax advantages compared to other types of income. In numerous countries, such as the United States, they usually entice reduced tax rates compared to standard income. For small business owners, this difference can lead to significant tax savings. In the United States, individuals pay taxes on long-term capital gains at preferential rates, which vary based on income.

- **Exit Strategy:** When small business owners plan their exit strategy, selling their business becomes a key consideration. If they trade their business at a profit, the resulting capital gains can create a substantial retirement nest egg or offer a financial buffer for future ventures.

- Investors frequently gravitate toward businesses with a

track record of growth and profitability, as these qualities often signal potential for capital gains. Demonstrating such a history can make it easier for you to attract investors seeking opportunities to achieve capital gains on their investments.

Consider the scenario where you launch a tech start-up and draw in investors who buy shares in your venture. As your business flourishes and becomes more successful, the shares' worth escalates. When these investors sell their shares later at a higher price, they earn profits as capital gains. This scenario rewards your initial backers financially and injects additional capital into your business, offering continued expansion and development opportunities.

Calculating Capital Gains Tax

You need to grasp a few key concepts to calculate the capital gains tax for your small business. Essentially, this tax applies to the profit you earn from selling an asset, such as your business. The tax amount you're responsible for varies based on factors such as how long you've owned the asset, your business structure, location, and any available exemptions. For instance, a tech entrepreneur in Massachusetts who has succeeded is more likely to encounter a higher capital gain tax rate than the owner of a modest bookstore in Maine.

- **Ownership Duration:** If your business ownership exceeds one year, you could be eligible for the more favorable long-term capital gain tax rates, generally lower than the ordinary income rates. The tax treatment for short-term gains resembles that of regular income, while long-term gains use tax rates of either 0%, 15%, or 20%, depending on your income bracket (Orem, 2024).

- **Business Structure:** Your business structure directly influences capital gain tax calculations because different structures have distinct tax regulations. Sole proprietorships and partnerships typically pass profits directly to owners, affecting individual tax rates. In contrast, corporations may face separate taxation, possibly leading to double taxation on profits. Therefore, understanding your structure's tax implications is crucial for accurate capital gains assessment.

- **Exemptions:** Certain exemptions, such as the Section 1202 Exemption, offer relief for qualified small business stock (QSBS) in the United States. Depending on the situation, you can exclude as much as 100% of the profit from selling QSBS from federal taxation. Additionally, retirement exemptions and rollover reliefs provide opportunities to substantially decrease your tax obligations (*Capital Gains Tax on Small Business Sale*, 2023).

To calculate your capital gains tax, start by figuring out your profit. This profit is the gap between your business's selling price and its adjusted basis. The adjusted basis includes the original cost of the business as well as any enhancements and modifications made over time. Once you have this figure, apply the relevant tax rates based on your income bracket and the duration of ownership.

For instance, if you are single and your income is between $44,626 and $492,300, your long-term capital gains tax rate would be 15%. If your income exceeds $492,300, the rate increases to 20%. The thresholds differ based on different filing statuses, such as married filing jointly, married filing separately, and head of household (*2023 Capital Gains Rates*, n.d.).

Remember that the nuances of capital gains tax can be intricate. Small business proprietors should grasp the intricacies of capital gains tax and adeptly handle it, as it can profoundly impact their financial results when selling their business.

Moreover, capital gains tax operates independently from income tax, ensuring that capital gains don't add to your total taxable income. As a coffee shop owner in Seattle, you'll need to calculate the capital gains tax separately from the taxes on your business earnings. Understanding this difference is vital for accurately calculating your financial responsibilities.

Minimizing Capital Gains Tax

As a small business owner, you're probably searching for efficient methods to reduce your capital gains tax liability. Here, we present a set of techniques that can help you:

- **Understand Capital Gains Tax Rates:** Familiarize yourself with the existing capital gains tax rates and brackets. If you anticipate a decrease in your income for the upcoming year, contemplate postponing the sale of assets to ensure they align with a lower tax bracket.

- **Use Tax-Advantaged Retirement Accounts:** Increase your contributions to retirement accounts such as 401(k)s, traditional IRAs, and Roth IRAs. These accounts offer tax deferral advantages for capital gains and dividends, significantly decreasing your present taxable earnings.

- **Implement Strategic Asset Location:** Allocate investments in a tax-efficient manner. Place assets generating significant taxable income, such as high-yield bonds, in tax-advantaged accounts, and keep less tax-intensive assets, such as index funds, in taxable accounts.

- **Apply Tax-Loss Harvesting Techniques:** To offset capital gains tax on your other investments, consider selling investments that aren't performing well. However, it's essential to adhere to the IRS's "wash-sale" rule, which prevents you from claiming a loss on a security if you buy a substantially identical security within 30 days before or after the sale (*What Strategies Can We Use?* n.d.).

- **Utilize Employee Retention and Sick and Family Leave Credits:** If your business was affected by COVID-19, you might be eligible for employee retention sick and family leave credits, which can reduce the amount you owe in taxes (Lewis, 2023).

- **Time Income:** Choose when to receive income wisely. Delaying or expediting income can help you manage your tax bracket and reduce your capital gains tax liability.

- **Reduce Adjusted Gross Income (AGI):** You can lower your AGI by contributing to health savings accounts or retirement plans, deducting home office expenses, and accounting for interest paid on business financing.

- **Optimize Retirement Savings Accounts:** Manage your retirement plans effectively and use Roth 401(k) choices to opt for immediate taxation.

- **Leverage Gift and Inheritance Tax Laws:** Understand and utilize tax laws related to gifts and inheritances to transfer assets tax-efficiently.

- **Hold Investments for Longer Than One Year:** You can pay less taxes on your investments if you keep them for over a year, as long-term capital gains tax rates are lower for holdings held longer than 12 months (Tamplin, 2024).

- **Stagger Selling of Investments:** You can maximize the advantages of lower long-term capital gains rates by staggering your asset sales across a period. Additionally, you can explore investing in index funds and employing tax-loss harvesting techniques to counterbalance the impact of elevated capital gains tax rates.

Tailoring your approach to your business's circumstances is crucial to successfully applying these strategies. We strongly advise you to consult a tax professional to ensure the proper implementation of these strategies and adherence to tax regulations. Remember that tax laws are complex and subject to change, so staying informed and obtaining expert guidance is critical to optimizing your tax planning.

Key Takeaways

- Capital gains are profits from selling assets such as stocks or real estate, with realized gains occurring upon sale and unrealized gains existing on paper.

- Small businesses benefit from capital gains through investment opportunities, tax advantages, aiding exit strategies, and attracting investors.

- Calculating capital gains tax involves understanding profit, ownership duration, business structure, and available exemptions. Rates vary by income bracket and ownership length.

- To minimize capital gains tax, understand tax rates, use tax-advantaged accounts, implement strategic asset location, apply tax-loss harvesting, consider employee retention credits, time income wisely, reduce AGI, optimize retirement savings, leverage gift and inheritance laws, hold investments longer, and stagger investment sales.

- It's important to customize each strategy according to your specific business circumstances. To ensure compliance and get the most out of these approaches, it's recommended that you seek guidance from a tax professional.

After delving into the fundamental aspects of capital gains and the strategies to reduce their tax implications, our attention now turns to another critical area: depreciation. For small business owners, it is imperative to comprehend and harness the potential of depreciation as it plays a pivotal role in securing substantial tax advantages. The upcoming chapter will explore maximizing depreciation to bolster your business's financial well-being.

Tyler Harrison's
Small Business Tax Hacks

Review Request Page

Free Goodwill

"Helping one person might not change the whole world, but it could change the world for one person." - Anonymous.

Hey there, friend!
You know that feeling when you hold the door open for someone, and they beam at you like you've just made their day? That's the kind of vibe we're talking about here. Helping someone out—especially when it comes to the sticky world of taxes—can be that little nudge that turns their day around. And who knows? It might just be the thing that changes their whole world.

I have a small favor to ask, and it won't cost you more than a minute or two. But to the person you help, it might just be priceless. Could you drop a few lines about your journey with this book? Your insights could light up the path for a fresh-faced entrepreneur stepping up to the plate, ready to hit a home run, or a customer conquering their business goals, one tax slip at a time. How about it? Ready to spread a little cheer and change a life? All you've got to do is share your story. It's as simple as that!

Leave a review here and share the knowledge you've gained below:

https://www.amazon.com/review/review-your-purchases/?asin=B0CZSF1Z7K

A huge, heartfelt thank you for being here. Now, let's dive back into our tax-tackling quest, shall we?

Cheering you on always,

Tyler Harrison

> PS: Also, did you know that when you share something truly helpful, your stock goes up in someone's world? Could this book be a gold mine for another small business champ? Pass the baton! Let's get those good vibes rolling!

STRATEGY 8-TURN TIME INTO MONEY BY DOMINATING DEPRECIATION

"Depreciation is not just a deduction; it's a strategic business advantage.

Making the Most of Depreciation

As a small business owner, you stand at the threshold of financial empowerment through mastering depreciation. This overlooked yet powerful tool is your key to unlocking substantial tax advantages. Understanding depreciation enhances financial literacy and transforms how you view your assets and investments.

Calculating depreciation can seem daunting, but we'll break down this process with clear guidance, gaining control over your business's financial future. Navigating IRS rules for claiming depreciation can be complex, yet it's crucial for optimizing your tax returns. Embrace this knowledge to make strategic decisions, avoid common pitfalls, and see the true impact of depreciation on your business finances. Your journey toward financial savvy and security begins here.

What It Is Depreciation and Why It Matters

Depreciation holds significant financial importance, impacting both businesses and individuals, as it signifies the gradual decrease in an asset's value over time. This concept matters for several reasons:

First, depreciation impacts financial statements, affecting a company's profitability and tax liabilities. Businesses must account for depreciation to reflect asset values and calculate expenses accurately. It's similar to acknowledging that a delivery van used in your catering business in Houston has a limited lifespan and deducts a portion of its cost annually.

Second, it's crucial to comprehend depreciation to make informed investment decisions. Investors need to evaluate how an asset's value decreases over time to gauge its long-term value accurately.

For instance, consider a company that purchases machinery for $100,000. Over five years, the machinery depreciates by $20,000 annually. Without accounting for depreciation, the company might overestimate its actual worth. As another example, a technology company in Silicon Valley can achieve substantial tax savings by correctly depreciating its servers and other technological equipment.

Depreciation is a fundamental financial concept with practical implications for businesses and investors. It affects financial statements, taxation, and investment decisions, making it crucial to grasp its nuances for economic success.

How to Calculate Depreciation

To calculate depreciation effectively, follow these steps:

1. **Select the Depreciation Method:** Choose the depreciation method that best aligns with your assets and financial objectives, such as straight-line, units of production, double declining balance, or sum of the years' digits.

2. **Gather Information:** Gather crucial information about the asset, including its initial cost, anticipated salvage value (the estimated value at the end of its useful life), and expected utility duration.

3. **Apply the Straight-Line Method:** To calculate depreciation using the straight-line method, subtract the salvage value from the asset's cost and divide the result by the asset's useful life. For instance, if you bought equipment for $20,000, it has a salvage value of $1,500, and its helpful life spans 10 years, the yearly depreciation amounts to ($20,000 - $1,500) / 10), resulting in $1,850.

4. **Consider Other Methods:** Explore other depreciation methods, such as double declining balances or the sum of the years' digits, which may be more suitable for specific

assets or tax purposes.

5. **Record Depreciation:** Accurately record annual depreciation expenses, as they will impact your financial statements and taxes.

6. **Adjust for Tax Rules:** Understand the tax rules related to depreciation, as the IRS has guidelines for depreciation on various assets.

7. **Seek Professional Advice:** If you're unsure or handling complex assets, seeking advice from a tax professional or accountant is smart. They can offer guidance tailored to the most recent tax laws.

Remember that depreciation plays a crucial role in your finances, enabling you to distribute asset costs over their useful life, thereby presenting a more precise reflection of their value on your financial records. To calculate depreciation accurately and in line with the latest tax guidelines, follow these steps diligently.

Pros And Cons Of The Different Depreciation Methods

Financial management requires that you know the pros and cons of various depreciation methods. Let's explore these methods:

- **Straight-Line Depreciation:** This method simplifies the process by dividing the asset's cost by expected years of use. It's easy to calculate and provides a consistent annual depreciation amount. However, it doesn't account for the actual rate at which an asset loses value, which might be more rapid in the early years of use. For example, if you purchase an assembly line for $60,000 with a salvage value of $10,000 and a useful life of 10 years, the annual depreciation expense is $5,000.

- **Declining Balance Method:** This approach speeds up the depreciation process during the initial stages of the asset's life, providing tax advantages by lowering taxable income during this period. However, its calculation is more complex, and the more significant upfront depreciation comes at the cost of more minor deductions in future years when your business may be in a higher tax bracket.

- **Sum-Of-The-Years Digits:** Similar to the declining balance, this method accelerates depreciation early in the asset's life, providing early tax benefits. The downside is the complexity of its calculations.

- **Units of Production Method:** This method calculates an asset's depreciation by estimating the number of units it will produce throughout its lifespan. It aligns depreciation with production quantity but assumes the asset depreciates evenly over its productive life, which might be accurate.

Each method has its trade-offs. The straight-line method is simple and predictable, ideal if you prefer consistent accounting. In contrast, declining balance or sum-of-the-years digits are more suited if you seek higher upfront tax deductions. Remember, the best method depends on your business needs and financial goals.

Also, be aware of Section 179 deductions, which allow immediate expensing of asset costs up to a specific limit, and bonus depreciation, enabling 100% deduction of the remaining basis in the first year (Shelton, 2023). Consider these factors when selecting a depreciation method because they can significantly affect your tax liabilities.

How to Claim Depreciation

To claim depreciation according to IRS rules, follow these essential steps:

- **Business or Income-Producing Activity:** To qualify for depreciation, the property must be used for business or income-generating purposes. The IRS specifies that assets used exclusively for personal activities cannot be depreciated.

- **Qualified Property:** After September 27, 2017, you can take advantage of an 80% special depreciation allowance for eligible assets acquired and put into service after December 31, 2022. This allowance is applicable after deducting any eligible Section 179 deduction and precedes any other permissible depreciation (*Topic No. 704, Depreciation*, n.d.).

- **Correct Amount of Depreciation:** To maximize your tax benefits, ensure you claim the appropriate amount of depreciation each tax year. Failing to do so can impact the deductions you're eligible for.

- **Documentation:** Collect comprehensive details regarding depreciable business assets, including the initial acquisition cost. You will require documentation such as the asset's purchase price, receipts, and the date it became operational within your business operations.

- **Types of Depreciable Property:** Small businesses can depreciate property used for business or investment purposes, including machinery, equipment, buildings, vehicles, and furniture.

- **Bonus Depreciation:** Stay vigilant about bonus depreciation regulations, as the IRS might permit extra first-year depreciation for specific assets. Verify if your property qualifies for this additional benefit (*Publication 946 (2022), How To Depreciate Property*, n.d.).

- **Reporting:** Accurately report your depreciation deductions on your tax return after each accounting year.

Understanding specific regulations and constraints is essential to avoid mistakes when calculating depreciation. For example, the IRS establishes guidelines regarding the commencement of asset depreciation, typically when placed into service, and imposes annual limits on the depreciation amount you can assert.

The Impact of Depreciation on Your Business Finances

To effectively plan your finances and devise a tax strategy, it's crucial to comprehend how depreciation directly influences your business.

Bonus Depreciation Phasing Out

In 2017, the Tax Cuts and Jobs Act (TCJA) ushered in a significant change by introducing a 100% bonus depreciation for specific assets, particularly advantageous for manufacturers and businesses heavily reliant on machinery and equipment. However, as of December 31, 2022, this bonus depreciation is gradually diminishing, decreasing by 20% annually until it reaches a complete phase-out by 2027. In 2023, the deduction stood at 80%, followed by a reduction to 60% in 2024, and so forth (*Depreciation Changes for 2023*, 2023).

Section 179 Deduction

Section 179 provides an alternative approach to depreciation, permitting you to deduct the expense of qualified assets during the initial year of use. In 2023, the highest deduction achievable through Section 179 is $1,160,000, gradually reducing as equipment acquisitions surpass $2,890,000 (*Impacts of the 2023 Bonus Depreciation Phase Out*, 2023).

Changes In Macrs Depreciation Method

The Modified Accelerated Cost Recovery System (MACRS) underwent revisions that affected the recovery periods of various asset types. The recovery period extension now applies to qualified improvement property and adjustments to the treatment of qualified film, television, and live theatrical productions.

Depreciation And Business Finances

These changes in depreciation rules can significantly influence your business's bottom line. They affect cash flow, net income, and financial ratios, influencing decisions such as capital investments and pricing strategies. The updated rules may also impact tax liabilities, increasing or decreasing them depending on your circumstances.

Real-Life Impacts

A manufacturing company that relies heavily on machinery faces the challenge of an upcoming decrease in bonus depreciation, potentially resulting in higher future tax liabilities. This situation calls for a reassessment of their asset acquisition and investment tactics. Conversely, companies capable of effectively leveraging Section 179 will benefit from the expanded deduction limits, resulting in substantial tax advantages, particularly for those procuring equipment that falls below the phase-out threshold.

Staying Compliant and Maximizing Benefits

Staying informed about these modifications is crucial, and collaborating closely with tax advisors is essential to comply with regulations and optimize tax advantages. It's important to remember that the state-level conformity with federal changes may differ, impacting your overall tax planning approach.

Making the Most of Depreciation

To make the most of depreciation in 2024, consider these strategic considerations:

- **Leverage Cost Segregation:** Cost segregation allows you to depreciate different components of commercial property within a shorter time frame than the standard 27.5 or 39 years used for residential and commercial properties (*The Cost Segregation Depreciation Guide for 2024*, n.d.). By doing so, you can claim more significant depreciation expenses in the initial years, reducing tax liability and enhancing cash flow. Hire an expert to assess and categorize assets such as personal property, land improvements, or real property, each with its distinct depreciation schedule.

- **Understand Equipment Depreciation:** Comprehend the factors determining equipment depreciation, such as wear and tear, obsolescence, and helpful lifespan. For instance, a laptop has a shorter useful life than a new truck due to rapid technological advancements. Remember, depreciation allows you to calculate profit from equipment more accurately and determine when it's time for replacement.

- **Stay Updated on Tax Rules:** Keep abreast of

changes in depreciation rules, such as adjustments in depreciation rates for specific assets and introducing new categories of depreciable assets. For example, the Tax Relief for American Families and Workers Act of 2024 includes 100% bonus depreciation (Waddell, 2024). Understanding these changes helps in optimizing tax strategy and cost savings.

- **Utilize MACRS:** The Modified Accelerated Cost Recovery System (MACRS) is a primary method of depreciation for federal income tax in the U.S. Anticipate changes to MACRS, such as altering the classification of certain property types or adjusting depreciation rates. Stay informed and revise your financial projections accordingly.

- **Choose the Right Depreciation Method:** Choose a method that aligns with your financial strategies, such as straight-line, declining balance, or production units. Each method has distinct implications for tax liability and your overall financial position.

You must actively implement these strategies to enhance financial performance and skillfully manage tax obligations.

Common Mistakes with Depreciation

In managing depreciation effectively, you must be vigilant to avoid these critical errors:

- **Depreciate Major Assets Correctly:** Don't just expense all purchases. Depreciate significant assets over their useful life as per MACRS guidelines. This ensures accurate tax benefits.

- **Match Asset to Depreciation Schedule:** Carefully assign assets to the proper depreciable life or method. For instance, don't depreciate a 15-year asset over just 5 years. This is crucial to avoid tax inaccuracies.

- **Distinguish Repairs from Depreciable Expenditures:** Recognize that some expenses are repairs and maintenance, not depreciable costs. Correctly categorizing these expenses avoids miscalculations in depreciation.

- **Understand Rental Property Depreciation:** With the increasing prevalence of rental properties, it's essential to grasp their specific depreciation requirements to avoid miscalculations.

- **Navigate Book vs. Tax Depreciation Differences:** Be aware that depreciation for financial reporting may differ from tax depreciation. Seek a skilled bookkeeper's guidance in these matters.

- **Handle Overhead Costs Accurately in Inventory:** Ensure correct application of overhead costs in inventory valuation. Mistakes here can skew balance sheet accuracy and year-end inventory figures.
- **Respect Legal Asset Life Limitations:** Acknowledge legal limits on asset life, particularly in leasing scenarios, to avoid depreciating assets over incorrect periods.
- **Accurately Assess Residual Values:** Don't underestimate the importance of correct residual value assessment, as it significantly impacts the depreciable amount and annual depreciation expenses.

It's also crucial to remember that depreciation lowers the worth of your assets listed on the balance sheet. Moreover, be updated with the latest regulations to align your strategies with your business needs.

Key Takeaways

- Depreciation is vital for reflecting actual asset values and tax liabilities and understanding its impact on financial statements and investments.

- To claim depreciation, follow the IRS guidelines and make sure the property is utilized for business purposes or generating income.

- Be aware of the phasing out of bonus depreciation and changes in Section 179 and MACRS, which will impact your business finances.

- Utilize strategies such as cost segregation and staying informed on tax rules to maximize depreciation benefits.

- Avoid common depreciation mistakes, such as incorrectly depreciating significant assets or misunderstanding rental property depreciation.

- Consult with tax professionals to align your strategies with current regulations and optimize your business's fiscal health.

Now that you've gained a solid grasp of the essential principles of depreciation and its crucial role in maximizing tax benefits for your small business, it's time to explore tax incentives in greater detail. The next chapter will uncover hidden opportunities to boost financial growth and secure stability.

STRATEGY 9-TAX CREDIT AS A FINANCIAL REWARDS

"Tax credits are the treasure trove many businesses overlook. Dive in and discover wealth.

Leveraging Tax Credits

Tax credits are your hidden arsenal for financial resilience as a small business owner. These incentives are not mere deductions but powerful tools that directly reduce your tax bill, fueling your mission. Imagine harnessing credits for hiring diverse talent, enhancing accessibility, or investing in health benefits.

Envision your business innovating or adopting sustainable energy, supported by the government's commitment to your success. Conserving cash isn't the sole focus here. It's about enabling your business to flourish in a competitive environment. Embrace this opportunity to transform your financial strategy and elevate your business.

Tax Credits vs Tax Deductions

As someone running a small business, it's essential to grasp how tax credits differ from tax deductions for your financial well-being. Here's a straightforward explanation:

Tax Credits: Tax credits are like getting a dollar back for every dollar you owe in taxes. Imagine you've earned a $1,000 tax credit; it cuts down your tax bill by that same $1,000. These credits are super valuable because they directly reduce your tax. You can get them by offering family and medical leave or investing in eco-friendly vehicles. They're an excellent method to save on taxes!

Tax Deductions: Tax deductions lower your taxable income based on your top federal income tax bracket. For example, if you fall into the 22% tax bracket, a deduction of $1,000 means you will save $220 in taxes. Remember, deductions trim down the income that will be taxed, not your actual tax bill (Orem, 2023).

In practice, a tax credit often significantly reduces your taxes owed compared to a deduction, but both are essential tools for tax savings. For instance, if your business spent money on certain types of equipment, you might qualify for deductions. However, if you hire individuals from certain target groups, you could be eligible for specific tax credits. For instance, you can get a maximum of $2,400 tax credit for every U.S. veteran you hire for full-time work (*The Ultimate Small Business Guide for Tax Season 2023*, 2023).

As you prepare to tackle your taxes, explore deductions and credits to boost your savings. Remember that teaming up with a tax expert can highlight the specific credits and deductions that fit your business's unique needs. It's all about making the most of your tax situation!

The Work Opportunity Tax Credit (WOTC)

As an entrepreneur, you can take advantage of the Work Opportunity Tax Credit (WOTC). This advantageous credit, nestled within the Internal Revenue Code, provides tax incentives for hiring from specific groups who often encounter employment hurdles, including veterans and long-term unemployed individuals. It's a win-win. You gain valuable team partners while producing a positive influence!

You can receive a credit worth 40% of the first-year wages paid to an eligible employee, up to $6,000. This means you could get up to $2,400 per employee! Even if the employee works less than 400 hours but at least 120 hours, you're still eligible for a 25% credit. For certain qualified veterans, this can go up to a whopping $24,000 in wages (Wood, 2023).

To claim the WOTC, you need to identify eligible employees and complete specific forms such as Form 8850. Remember, you must submit this form within 28 days of the employee's start date (*Work Opportunity Tax Credit*, n.d.). Don't let this opportunity slip; it's a win-win for your business and individuals seeking meaningful employment.

In 2022, State Workforce Agencies issued nearly 2.6 million WOTC certifications, highlighting its wide-reaching impact (Wood, 2023). Although there's a debate on its long-term effectiveness, studies suggest positive short-term employment gains for targeted groups. This incentive helps your business financially and fosters a more inclusive and diverse workforce.

The Disabled Access Credit

Guess what? There are fantastic tax perks for making your business disability-friendly! The Disabled Access Credit is your key to unlocking these benefits. You're in luck if your business raked in less than $1 million or had at most 30 full-time employees last year. You can snag a non-refundable credit, covering 50% of your eligible expenses for accessibility, with a maximum of $5,000 each year. It's a great way to enhance accessibility while easing your tax load (*Tax Tip 2023-66: Tax Benefits to Help Offset the Cost of Making Businesses Accessible to People With Disabilities*, n.d.). This includes ramps, modified restrooms, or specialized equipment for employees with disabilities.

To make your spaces friendlier to everyone, you can snag a tax deduction of up to $15,000 annually. This includes modifications such as lowering counters or enhancing wheelchair accessibility. Moreover, you can pair this deduction with the Disabled Access Credit, provided your expenses qualify for both perks. It's a win-win for inclusivity and your finances (*Tax Credits for Accommodating Disabled Workers*, 2023).

So, you're not only creating an inclusive environment for customers and employees but also getting a financial boost for doing so. Talk about a win-win! Don't miss out on these opportunities to improve your business and support a diverse community.

The Small Employer Health Insurance Premiums Credit

The Small Employer Health Insurance Premiums Credit can significantly cut your healthcare expenses. If your business employs fewer than 25 full-time equivalent workers, pays an average of under $50,000 annually, and provides a qualified health plan through the SHOP Marketplace, you're on the right track. Covering 50% of your employee-only healthcare costs is vital to unlocking this credit (*Small Business Health Care Tax Credit and the SHOP Marketplace*, 2023).

This is more than just receiving a tax break. This credit can reduce your healthcare expenses and ensure your team is well-covered. It's a win-win: simultaneously supporting your employees' health and saving cash.

So, if you're a small business owner scratching your head over healthcare costs, dive into this opportunity. More businesses can benefit from these credits, making it easier to provide quality health coverage without breaking the bank. Remember, healthy employees are happy, and happy employees are good for business!

Research and Experimentation Tax Credit

If you're a small business blazing trails in research and development, the revamped Research and Experimentation Tax Credit is your financial lifesaver. Thanks to the Inflation Reduction Act, the R&D tax credit now reaches an impressive $500,000 for eligible businesses, starting from tax years after December 31, 2022. For those with annual gross receipts under $5 million and no gross receipts in any of the five taxable years leading up to this year, this could mean significant tax relief for your innovative ventures (*Research & Experimental Expenses*, 2023).

Apart from increasing the payroll tax offset limit, the Tax Cuts and Jobs Act has changed how companies treat their research and experimental expenditures. These costs are not immediately expensed; they must be capitalized over five years for domestic activities or 15 years for international ones (*A Costly Situation for Businesses: Section 174 Capitalization Is Here*, 2023).

Navigating these changes might feel like rocket science, but it's worth it. Whether improving your products or developing new ones, these tax credits can provide the financial backing you need to keep innovating.

Energy Investment Tax Credit

Hey there, small business owners! Are you keen on going green and saving some green simultaneously? The Energy Investment Tax Credit (ITC) is your ticket to do just that. This fantastic opportunity, brought to life by the Inflation Reduction Act of 2022, is like a golden ticket for businesses like yours to invest in renewable energy and reap the rewards.

The ITC provides a base credit of 6% for your qualifying investment, skyrocketing to 30% for projects meeting specific requirements. And guess what? If you use all American-made steel and iron and a good chunk of U.S.-manufactured products, you're looking at a whopping 40% credit (*Inflation Reduction Act Energy Tax Credits*, 2023).

Investing in solar panels, wind turbines, or hydrogen power can slash your energy costs and contribute to a sustainable future, offering a win-win scenario for your business and the planet.

Latch on the new business opportunities and transform your business into an eco-friendly and financially intelligent enterprise. Embrace the strength of solar and wind power and government incentives to light the way to a prosperous future for your business!

Key Takeaways

- Tax credits directly slash your tax bill dollar for dollar, while tax deductions lower the portion of your taxable income, giving you a financial edge.

- By hiring individuals from specific groups, your business can benefit from the Work Opportunity Tax Credit (WOTC), potentially earning up to $2,400 for each eligible employee.

- Through the Disabled Access Credit, you can get a maximum of $5,000 non-refundable credit to make your business more accessible to individuals with disabilities.

- The Small Employer Health Insurance Premiums Credit can significantly reduce health care costs for businesses with less than 25 employees.

- The Research and Experimentation Tax Credit, especially beneficial for small businesses, supports innovative activities with a tax credit of up to $500,000.

- The Energy Investment Tax Credit encourages investments in renewable energy with a base credit of 6%, increasing up to 40% for qualifying projects.

Having discovered these valuable tax credits, get ready for tax season. Our next chapter leads you through organizing and maximizing your benefits. Now's the moment to transform these insights into practical actions for your business's financial prosperity!

STRATEGY 10-DETERMINE YOUR SEASONAL STRATEGY FOR FILLING YOUR TAX

"Tax season is not a time of year, but a state of mind. Prepare, plan, and prevail.

How to Prepare for Tax Season

Tax season can be a formidable challenge, yet it's a crucial part of your entrepreneurial journey. Imagine the peace of mind of having your financial records impeccably organized, every business expense validated, and payroll information thoroughly reviewed.

Think of the confidence you'll gain by double-checking deductions and credits, ensuring you're not leaving money on the table. Picture yourself smoothly preparing tax forms, adeptly planning for future payments, and the reassurance of consulting with a tax professional. This is your guide to mastering the tax season, turning a complex task into an empowering achievement.

Organizing Your Financial Records

Small businesses must organize financial records for tax season because it's about meeting regulations and making wise financial decisions. Well-maintained and structured financial records are fundamental for adequate tax preparation. They guarantee accurate tax payments and enable the discovery of possible deductions and credits, reducing tax obligations.

Missed tax deadlines can lead to penalties. Keeping thorough records helps you meet deadlines for income tax filings, quarterly taxes, payroll taxes, and more. Plus, separating personal and business finances is a must. This separation provides legal protection, accounting clarity, and easier tax reporting.

Effective record-keeping extends beyond taxation, benefiting decision-making by offering valuable insights into cash flow, profitability, and overall financial well-being. This foresight enables the establishment of attainable objectives and the development of strategies to address future requirements. Furthermore, small businesses encounter distinct tax-related circumstances, necessitating comprehension of current tax regulations, optimization of deductions, and exploration of pertinent tax incentives. These actions are pivotal in transforming tax season from a source of stress to a financially advantageous endeavor.

Take the plunge, start the organization process, and discover how arranging your receipts and invoices can simplify your tax season concerns and position your business for lasting prosperity. Remember that it's not solely about ensuring compliance but also about demonstrating financial understanding and optimizing your business's capabilities.

Verifying Your Business Expenses

Come tax season, it's crucial to get your ducks in a row, especially when verifying your business expenses. Every expense you claim affects your taxable income, so knowing what's deductible and what's not is essential.

First and foremost, remember the fundamental principle: Your expenses should be both typical for your industry and essential for your business. Remote operation encompasses office supplies, legal expenses, ongoing professional education, and home office expenditures.

If you're investing in new assets or property for your business, you should know about the phasing out the 100% bonus depreciation deduction starting in 2023. It's dropping to 80% this year and will decrease each year until 2027 (*Business Tax Changes You Need to Know*, 2023). Also, keep an eye on your employees' salary reductions and medical savings accounts—they've got new limits, too.

Remember, some business losses could qualify for tax deductions when you explore innovative products or services. This can provide valuable support in case your ventures encounter unexpected challenges.

Accurately managing your business expenses can substantially decrease your tax liability. The key lies in staying well-informed and maintaining proper organization. If you feel inundated, reaching out to a tax professional is wise. They can assist you in navigating this process and optimizing your deductions.

Reviewing Payroll Information

As a small business owner, conducting a thorough review of payroll information during tax season is essential. This process goes beyond tax compliance; it is pivotal in optimizing financial well-being. Start by identifying which employees are liable for payroll taxes and assess their taxable earnings. This evaluation should encompass regular wages, salaries, bonuses, and pre-tax deductions such as contributions to retirement plans and health insurance premiums.

Promptly filing payroll taxes is crucial. Small businesses usually have to submit several tax forms annually, including the business tax return, Forms W-2 and W-3 for employees, Form 1099-NEC for contractors, Form 940 along with fourth-quarter FUTA taxes, and either the quarterly Form 941 tax return or the annual Form 944 (*2023 Year-End Payroll & Tax Checklist*, 2023).

To simplify this procedure, keep precise payroll documentation year-round. This ensures compliance with deadlines and simplifies tax preparation. Furthermore, it would help if you learned about state and local minimum wage rate changes, as authorities have announced adjustments in response to inflation trends.

For effective tax planning and preparation, begin organizing your finances well in advance, ideally around mid-November. This proactive approach lets you assess your tax situation realistically before the year concludes, avoiding last-minute inaccuracies or oversights.

To maintain compliance with payroll tax regulations, it's vital to consistently assess and enhance your payroll procedures to guarantee precision and adherence. Contemplate delegating payroll tax responsibilities to expert firms or utilizing dependable payroll software for precise calculations and punctual submissions.

Reviewing payroll information during tax season is essential for ensuring compliance, financial stability, and maximizing potential tax benefits for small businesses. Stay proactive, organized, and informed about tax law changes to navigate this critical period effectively.

Double-Checking Deductions and Credits

As a small business owner, it's vital to grasp the significance of scrutinizing deductions and credits as tax season approaches. Tax credits act as incentives for participating in activities that align with government priorities, such as research and development, offering employee benefits, and investing in low-income communities. Unlike deductions, which decrease your taxable income, tax credits directly reduce your taxes.

In 2024, small business owners can benefit from several tax credits and deductions. One example is the Section 179 deduction, which allows businesses to deduct the cost of eligible equipment and property in the year of purchase, with a maximum limit of $1,160,000. Furthermore, the qualified business income deduction enables entities such as proprietorships and S corporations to deduct a portion of their business earnings, amounting to a maximum of 20% (*Deductions and Credits for Individuals and Small Businesses in Tax Season 2024*, 2023).

You can continue to be eligible for the Employee Retention Credit by claiming wages disbursed between March 13, 2020, and December 31, 2021, even though it no longer pertains to wages in the present (Johnson, 2023). Other significant deductions include those for home office expenses, business vehicles, and employee benefit programs.

Moreover, it's important to note the changes in income tax rates and brackets for 2024. Understanding these changes can help you plan better for your tax obligations.

These deductions and credits can significantly decrease your tax liability, enhancing your business's financial well-being. Nevertheless, due to the intricate nature of tax regulations, it is recommended that you collaborate with an informed tax expert to guarantee that you are fully capitalizing on these possibilities. Taking this proactive stance can result in significant cost reductions and adherence to tax legislation, ultimately positively impacting your business's profitability.

Preparing Your Tax Forms

As a small business owner, ensuring accurate and timely completion of your tax forms is crucial. Various business structures have distinct tax forms and deadlines, including sole proprietorships, partnerships, S corporations, and C corporations. For instance, C corporations, taxed separately from their owners, must submit IRS Form 1120 by April 15, 2024, whereas S corporations should file IRS Form 1120-S by March 15, 2024 (*What Business Owners Need to Know*, 2024).

Understanding the tax responsibilities your business must meet is vital. These include excise taxes, employment taxes, self-employment taxes, estimated taxes, and income taxes. The exact tax amounts and reporting requirements vary based on your business's structure. For example, C corporations face taxation on profits and dividends, whereas entities such as sole proprietorships and S corporations, referred to as "flow-through" entities, report income individually.

Be aware of the critical deadlines, collect all required tax paperwork, and carefully assess potential tax credits and deductions, as they can substantially influence your tax liability. You can choose from various filing methods, such as traditional paper filing, utilizing online software, or enlisting the assistance of a professional tax consultant.

Adequate tax preparation enables you to avoid penalties, reduce tax burdens, and adhere to intricate tax regulations. Seeking guidance from a tax expert is recommended for skillful navigation of these complexities and enhancing your tax results.

Planning for Future Tax Payments

Planning for future tax payments is crucial for small businesses, especially in light of recent tax reforms and economic changes. The 2024 Tax Reform significantly overhauled the U.S. tax code, affecting small businesses in various ways. A fundamental change was reducing corporate tax rates, allowing small businesses to retain more profits.

The introduction of a 20% deduction for pass-through entities offers substantial tax savings. Still, it comes with restrictions and complex regulations (*How Does the 2024 Tax Reform Affect Year-End Tax Planning?* n.d.).

Adjusting to these changes requires reevaluating traditional tax planning strategies. For instance, the increased Section 179 limit to $1 million allows businesses to write off certain capital assets immediately, and the extension of 100% bonus depreciation through 2024 encourages significant capital investments. However, businesses should carefully consider their income situation and plan when applying for these benefits (*How Does the 2024 Tax Reform Affect Year-End Tax Planning?* n.d.).

Moreover, small businesses now face restrictions on deductions such as interest expenses and limitations on net operating losses (NOLs) carryback. These changes necessitate a reassessment of tax strategies to optimize tax savings.

Consulting a Tax Professional

Consulting a tax professional is crucial for small businesses, especially in 2024. Recent changes in tax regulations, such as increased standard deductions, revised mileage rates, and new employer tax credits, make staying compliant and minimizing financial burdens more challenging.

Tax consultants offer comprehensive services, including tax planning, compliance, preparation, and strategic guidance tailored to business needs. They can help maximize tax savings, minimize liabilities, and ensure compliance with tax laws, freeing business owners to focus on growth.

In selecting the right tax advisor, look for certified professionals experienced in business taxes, such as enrolled agents, certified public accountants, or specialized attorneys. A qualified advisor should know about small business and industry-related tax laws. To find a reputable tax advisor, start with referrals from trusted business professionals or consult professional tax organizations.

Leveraging the expertise of a tax professional is essential for small businesses in 2024 to navigate complex tax changes, maximize benefits, and focus on business growth.

Key Takeaways

- Accurate recordkeeping helps meet tax deadlines, separates personal and business finances, and improves decision-making.

- Small businesses must grasp tax regulations, deductions, and credits to reduce their tax obligations effectively.

- Examining payroll data, timely tax filing, and upholding precise recordkeeping are vital for ensuring compliance.

- Leveraging tax credits and deductions can significantly reduce tax bills and improve financial health.

- Preparing tax forms correctly and on time is crucial, with specific forms and deadlines based on business structure.

- Planning for future tax payments requires adapting to recent tax reforms and consulting a tax professional for optimal tax efficiency.

After diligently preparing your small business for tax season, it's essential to know the next crucial step: understanding the tax audit process. In the next chapter, we'll discuss the intricacies of tax audits, ensuring you're well-prepared to handle any potential challenges.

STRATEGY 11-FORTIFY AGAINST FISCAL AUDIT FEARS

"An audit is not an end but a new beginning. Embrace it, learn from it, and emerge stronger.

Tax Audit Process

When facing a tax audit, it can feel like navigating uncharted waters, fraught with uncertainty and anxiety. This journey, however, is not one you must embark on alone. Understand that audits are standard procedures, often triggered by common discrepancies or random selections. Preparation is your strongest ally.

By adopting best practices, you can approach this process with confidence and clarity. Responding to an audit is crucial as it can significantly affect the outcome. Knowing the dos and don'ts in handling audits can make a big difference. Finally, learn from the experience. Implementing preventive measures ensures your future financial journey is smoother and more secure. Your resilience and proactive approach will safeguard your business's legacy.

Auditing- What It Is and Why It Happens

An IRS audit involves examining an organization or individual's financial records and information to confirm accurate reporting per tax laws and validate the accuracy of the reported tax amount. For various reasons, small businesses may attract IRS audits, and it's essential to understand these triggers to prepare adequately.

The IRS may audit your small business for various common reasons:

- **Cash-Intensive Business:** If your business, such as a restaurant, convenience store, or construction company, regularly receives or makes cash payments, it could be more likely to get audited. This is because cash transactions are more complex to trace and may lead to underreported income.

- **Child Care Business:** Many businesses frequently fail to report their income accurately, exaggerate their expenses, deal in cash transactions, and maintain inadequate records, which increases their susceptibility to audits.

- **Vehicle Deductions:** A common trigger for overstating deductions is claiming actual costs and mileage expenses when only one can be claimed. It's crucial to maintain adequate records in this regard.

- **Meal, Travel, and Entertainment Deductions:** Claiming these deductions for expenses with no business purpose or poor record keeping can lead to scrutiny.

- **Home Office Deduction:** Many people incorrectly claim this deduction for spaces not regularly and exclusively used for business or need proper documentation.

- **Low Wage With S Corp Election:** Misconceptions about reducing tax bills through specific business structures can attract audits.

- **Earned Income Tax Credit:** Incorrectly reporting self-employment income to claim this credit can be a red flag.

- **Paycheck Protection Loan Recipient:** Misuse of these loans can lead to audits, as the IRS checks for proper usage of the funds.

- **Reporting Only a Part of the Annual Income:** Omitting income sources in your tax return is a significant trigger for an IRS audit.

- **Unusual Charity Donations:** Disproportionate charitable contributions compared to annual income can attract attention.

- **Excessive Self-Employment Tax Deductions:** Claiming

deductions not applicable to personal expenses and overstating deductions can be problematic.

- **Hobby vs. Business:** The IRS scrutinizes businesses that do not show a net profit in three out of five years, suspecting it might be a hobby.

- **Foreign Financial Assets:** Holding significant funds in foreign accounts can trigger an audit.

- **Investment Income Omissions:** Not reporting or underreporting investment income is a standard audit cause.

- **Bitcoin and NFT Transactions:** The IRS closely monitors the increase in digital asset transactions.

As a small business owner, understanding the IRS audit process and the reasons behind the increased focus on small businesses can help you prepare and avoid an audit. Remember, being selected for an audit doesn't necessarily mean a problem; it's a process to ensure tax compliance.

Preparing for an Audit

Preparing for an audit constitutes a crucial element of small business management. Below, we outline essential strategies to guarantee your readiness:

1. **React Promptly to the IRS Audit Letter:** If you receive an IRS audit letter, the first action is to contact the revenue agent for additional preparation time. Typically, you'll have 10 days from the letter's receipt. Still, requesting an extension of 30 to 60 days is advisable to thoroughly gather the necessary documents (*Your Checklist to Prepare for IRS Audits*, 2023).

2. **Engage With Your CPA:** Contact your certified public accountant (CPA) and secure a copy of your tax return. It's essential to gather all records supporting the figures on your return during this step. If you prepared the tax return, ensure you have the copy ready.

3. **Gather Essential Documents:** Ensure you organize the following records before the audit date.

    - **Proof of Income** includes W-2s, 1099s, and other income documents.
    - **Receipts and Records of Expenses:** These cover business expenses, charitable donations, medical costs, and more.
    - **Bank Statements:** These are used to verify deposits and withdrawals.
    - **Investment Records:** This includes stock or bond certificates and brokerage statements.

- o **Business Records:** Business operation documents include ledgers, invoices, and other essential paperwork.

- o **Home Office Expenses:** If claiming a home office deduction, prepare utility bills, mortgage/rent payments, etc.

- o **Vehicle Expenses:** This includes maintenance receipts, gas receipts, and business mileage logs.

- o **Retirement Plan Contributions:** Include contribution receipts and employer contribution records.

- o **Charitable Contributions:** Include receipts from charities and relevant bank statements.

4. **Reconcile Financial Statements:** Ensure your financial statements accurately represent your business's economic position. Regular reconciliation is crucial for maintaining audit-ready books.

5. **Understand the Audit Process:**
   A. **Initial Contact:** The IRS sends a letter requesting specific documents and records.
   B. **Examination of Records:** This happens either through mail or in person.
   C. **Closing Conference:** This happens either by phone or in-person to discuss findings.
   D. **Outcome:** The audit could result in no change, agreed changes (with possible penalties and fees), or disagreed changes leading to further proceedings.

6. **Communicate Effectively With Auditors:** Clear

communication with auditors is essential. Provide all necessary information and help them understand your business operations.

7. **Utilize Audit Findings for Improvement:** Use the findings to enhance your business practices post-audit. Implement recommendations to improve financial health and operational efficiency.

8. **Maintain Compliance:** Stay updated on the ever-changing tax regulations within your industry. It's crucial to have a consistent procedure for tax reporting and ensure you meet tax filing and payment deadlines. It's worth contemplating the assistance of a tax expert specializing in your industry.

9. **Separate Business and Personal Expenses:** Separating your business transactions by using a dedicated bank account and credit card is essential for effectively tracking deductions and credits associated with your business activities.

10. **Secure Electronic Records:** Invest in secured cloud storage or digital accounting software. QuickBooks or Zoho Books are excellent for simplifying the recordkeeping process. You can quickly produce the necessary documents during the audit. Regularly back up digital records and implement access controls and encryption.

11. **Document All Transactions:** Keep detailed documentation of all business dealings, encompassing financial records, receipts, and invoices. Employing a chronological recordkeeping system simplifies the tracking of economic activities.

12. **Build a Solid Defense Strategy:** Gather evidence

such as receipts, invoices, and bank statements. Seek legal and financial advice and maintain open communication with the IRS.

13. **Prepare for the Audit Interview:** Select a representative, practice responses, and review your case thoroughly before the interview.

14. **Deal With the Audit Outcome:** Understand the potential outcomes of an audit: your taxes may remain unchanged, you might owe additional taxes, or you may need to engage in an appeals process. If you owe additional taxes, explore available payment options to address this obligation.

Remember, an audit is more than a regulatory obligation. It's an opportunity better to understand your business's financial health and operational efficiency. By following these practices, you can turn an audit into a constructive experience for your business.

Responding to an Audit: Dos and Don'ts

When facing an audit, small businesses should approach the process strategically. Here are some fundamental dos and don'ts:

Dos

- **View From the Auditor's Perspective:** Consider what would interest an auditor and prepare accordingly.

- **Show Reality:** Don't "prepare" your company for the audit by masking the actual state of affairs. Be transparent and honest.

- **Understand the Audit Requirements:** To become acquainted with the audit plan, understand what the auditor intends to scrutinize.

- **Provide Direct Answers:** Respond concisely to the auditor's questions, avoiding unnecessary stories or elaborations.

- **Be Knowledgeable About Audit Criteria:** Ask the auditor to clarify if you're unsure about a potential nonconformity.

- **Stay Calm and Professional:** Answer the questions directly, and if there's something you don't know, admit it.

- **Know Your Processes:** Understand your role and how it relates to the broader quality management system.

Don'ts

- **Avoid Over-Preparing or Altering Reality:** Auditors aim to see the authentic state of your business.

- **Don't Be Overly Verbose:** Provide clear, relevant information without exceeding what is required.

- **Avoid Making Assumptions:** Ask for clarification if you know what a question means.

- **Don't Try to Impress With Jargon:** Stick to what you know and how it pertains to your business processes.

- **Avoid Surprises:** Be upfront about any potential issues that might affect the audit.

- **Don't Provide Unrequested Information:** If you're unsure about the relevance of specific data, consult with internal audit teams first.

Small businesses can effectively navigate the auditing process by adhering to these guidelines. Remember, an audit is not just a compliance exercise; it's an opportunity to improve and validate the integrity of your business operations.

After the Audit: Next Steps and Preventive Measures

As a small business owner, it's crucial to understand the aftermath of an audit and how to take preventive steps for the future. Here's a comprehensive guide to help you navigate post-audit actions and implement adequate preventative measures:

Post-Audit Actions

- **Review Audit Findings:** Thoroughly examine the auditor's report to pinpoint any non-compliance or errors in your financial records. This presents a valuable chance to comprehend the nature of the issues and the reasons behind them.

- **Rectify Errors:** If the audit uncovers any errors, immediately correct them. If required, make amendments to your tax returns and settle any additional taxes or penalties that may arise.

- **Improve Internal Controls:** Enhance your accounting procedures by introducing mechanisms for verification and balance to avert future mistakes. Consistently conducting internal audits is valuable, offering benefits beyond legal conformity, including overseeing your business activities and administration.

- **Ensure Compliance:** After the audit concludes, it's crucial to grasp the findings comprehensively, adhere to the auditor's determinations, and settle any extra tax, interest, or penalties as necessary.

- **Follow-Up With the IRS:** If you've made any adjustments following the audit, inform the IRS. Keeping open lines of communication can help build trust and may be beneficial in the future.

Preventive Measures For Future Audits

- **Maintain Accurate Records:** Maintain thorough and orderly documentation of every business transaction.

- **Understand Tax Obligations:** Stay updated on tax laws relevant to your business and consult experts if needed.

- **Report Income and Expenses Accurately:** Ensure your reported income aligns with official documents and avoid exaggerating expenses.

- **Make Estimated Tax Payments:** Pay estimated taxes quarterly if they apply to you to avoid penalties.

- **Seek Professional Help:** Hire a tax professional for complex business matters.

- **Avoid Common Audit Triggers:** Be cautious of large deductions and continual losses that might attract audits.

- **Conduct Regular Self-Audits:** Conduct periodic self-checks to identify and resolve issues early on.

By following these steps and staying vigilant about your business finances, you can mitigate the risks of future audits and ensure a smoother operational flow for your small business. Remember, transparency and accuracy in financial dealings are not just best practices but are essential for the longevity and credibility of your business.

John's Experience With an IRS Audit

John, a small business owner, recently faced a state audit. Initially overwhelmed, he embraced the challenge with a proactive mindset. Meticulously, John gathered his financial records, demonstrating commendable organization. His diligent bookkeeping paid off; the audit revealed only minor discrepancies. John swiftly addressed these, showcasing his commitment to compliance and transparency.

This experience was transformative for John. He emerged more knowledgeable about tax regulations and strengthened his business's financial practices. His story is an inspiring example for fellow entrepreneurs, emphasizing the importance of thorough record-keeping and a positive approach to regulatory scrutiny.

Key Takeaways

- Audits are essential for small businesses to ensure compliance with regulations and manage risks, especially in a dynamic business environment.

- Adequate audit preparation includes understanding different audit types, organizing financial records, and maintaining consistent compliance.

- Responding to an audit requires viewing the process from the auditor's perspective, providing direct and honest answers, and understanding audit criteria.

- Post-audit actions involve reviewing findings, correcting errors, improving internal controls, and communicating with the IRS.

- Preventive measures for future audits include maintaining accurate records, understanding tax obligations, accurately reporting income and expenses, and conducting regular self-audits.

- As a business owner, you should embrace audits as opportunities for improvement, consistently update your tax strategies, and proactively keep abreast of tax law changes to prevent future audits.

Having navigated the complexities of a tax audit, you're

now more equipped than ever. But the journey doesn't end here. Next, we'll discuss how you can ensure your business remains adaptable and compliant amidst constantly evolving tax regulations.

STRATEGY 12-GUIDE YOUR JOURNEY THROUGH CHANGING TAX LAWS

"Change in tax laws is the only constant. Stay illuminated, stay ahead.

Staying Updated With Tax Law Changes

The ever-shifting terrain of tax laws requires agility and foresight. Rapid and substantial changes can significantly affect your business's financial well-being. Not staying updated isn't only a missed opportunity but can also lead to costly mistakes. Thankfully, you're not alone. There are dependable resources to guide you through these complexities.

Embracing new tax laws can unlock potential benefits, fostering growth and stability. Overcoming hesitations is crucial. Remember, adapting to changes in tax law is about more than just compliance. Seize opportunities to strengthen and propel your business forward in this ever-changing economic landscape.

An Ever-Changing Landscape as the Nature of Tax Laws

When a new government administration comes into power, tax laws often change, reflecting the new administration's policy priorities and economic agenda. This can significantly impact small businesses.

For instance, the Biden administration's tax plan proposes substantial changes to corporate tax laws, potentially raising corporate tax rates and modifying tax benefits available under current law. These changes are part of a broader effort to balance the tax code, which some perceive as skewed towards large corporations and wealthy individuals, as seen with the 2017 Tax Cuts and Jobs Act. This act, passed under a different administration, included significant revisions to the U.S. international corporate tax system and lowered the corporate income tax rate from 35% to 21% (Cole, 2024).

Small businesses can experience a direct impact from alterations in tax laws. Increased corporate tax rates may affect a small business's bottom line, requiring budgeting and financial planning adjustments. Conversely, reductions in tax rates or new tax incentives can provide financial relief and opportunities for growth. For example, the CARES Act, introduced in response to the COVID-19 pandemic, provided significant financial support to small businesses through various tax reliefs and incentives (*Emergency Relief for Small Businesses*, n.d.).

Small business owners must stay informed about tax law changes and understand how they impact their business operations and financial strategies.

The Impact of Not Staying Updated

Failure to keep up with the latest tax laws can result in non-compliance, potentially leading to penalties or missing out on opportunities to save on taxes. For instance, a new 3.8% small business surtax on S corporations, partnerships, and LLCs earning business income started in 2024 (*The New Tax Laws*, 2022). Unawareness of such updates could result in unexpected tax liabilities.

Moreover, small businesses often face higher effective tax rates than larger companies. Research shows entrepreneurs pay up to 10% more tax as a percentage of profits than big businesses, burdening newer companies more (Thomas-Bryant, 2018).

Compliance with sales and use tax can also be challenging, especially in new technologies such as cryptocurrency and NFTs. States continually adapt their tax policies to include such developments, and businesses need to stay informed to remain compliant.

The cost of compliance is another concern. Small businesses manually managing compliance activities spend significant amounts monthly on tax-related tasks, from rate calculations to exemption certificate management. You can mitigate this financial burden by keeping up-to-date with tax laws and implementing effective tax management strategies.

Staying educated about tax law updates is essential for small businesses. It not only helps avoid penalties and audits but also ensures that the business takes advantage of all available tax benefits, ultimately contributing to its financial health and growth.

Reliable Resources for Staying Updated

As a small business owner, staying updated with tax laws is critical for compliance and financial planning. You can consult these trustworthy sources for assistance:

- **Internal Revenue Service (IRS)—Tax Reform Small Business Initiative:** This section of the IRS website provides comprehensive information on tax reforms affecting small businesses, including deductions, depreciation, expensing, and new tax laws. It compares pre- and post-tax cuts and Jobs Act scenarios to help you understand the changes.

- **IRS—Small Business and Self-Employed Tax Center:** This wealth of suggestions can provide valuable information for small business owners. It covers diverse subjects, from filing and paying taxes to learning credits and deductions. The center also provides popular forms and instructions, such as Form 1040, W-9, and Form 941, essential for small business tax compliance.

- **IRS—Tools and Resources for Small Businesses:** The IRS also offers various tools and resources specifically designed to assist small businesses. These include tax tips, news releases, fact sheets, e-news subscriptions, and guidance on various tax-related issues. This platform is handy for keeping abreast of the most recent tax updates and how they affect your business.

- **Tax Foundation:** This organization is renowned for its comprehensive analysis and transparent reporting on tax policy. They provide in-depth research and education on tax policies, helping you understand the what and why of tax law changes. This understanding is crucial for planning and adapting your business strategies accordingly.

- **Bloomberg Tax:** This resource stands out for its real-time updates and expert insights into tax law developments. Their extensive coverage offers both news and practical guidance on how changes may affect your business. Utilize this source to manage intricate tax situations or identify chances to enhance your tax position.

- **Accounting Today:** This website is a trusted source for accountants and business owners, offering news, analysis, and expert opinions on tax law changes. Accounting Today provided detailed guidance and insights in response to complex tax reforms such as the Tax Cuts and Jobs Act of 2017, which helps businesses understand the implications and prepare effectively.

Remember, the tax landscape for small businesses is

constantly evolving. Regularly consulting these resources can help you stay informed and make sound financial decisions for your business. Whether you're grappling with new deductions, trying to understand complex tax reforms, or simply keeping up with filing requirements, these authoritative sources support you every step of the way.

Making the Most of New Tax Laws

When tax laws change, they frequently introduce fresh chances for saving on taxes. Keeping yourself informed allows you to seize these opportunities and lower the amount of taxes you owe. Therefore, you must be proactive in making the most of the new tax laws for your small business. Here are ways you can actualize this feat:

- **Understand the Changes:** Key tax changes include increased standard deductions, revised mileage rates, and new employer tax credits. The Tax Relief for American Families and Workers Act of 2024 also introduces business tax relief, enhanced child tax credits, and support for small businesses (*Understanding the Tax Relief for American Families and Workers Act*, 2024).

- **Maximize Deductions and Credits:** Leverage the increased standard deductions to reduce taxable income. For single filers, the deduction is now $13,600, and for married couples filing jointly, it's $27,200 (*3 Tax Changes for Small Businesses*, 2024). Also, take advantage of the new employer tax credits for benefits such as paid family and medical leave.

- **Utilize Enhanced Child Tax Credits:** If your business is a family affair, the expanded child tax credits can be beneficial. These credits have been adjusted for inflation and increased refundability, offering more financial assistance to families.

- **Adapt to Reporting Threshold Adjustments:** Businesses using subcontract labor now benefit from a revised reporting threshold, which reduces administrative burdens and streamlines operations.

- **Consult With a Tax Professional:** A tax professional can guide you through these changes and ensure your business complies with the latest laws while maximizing tax benefits.

- **Stay Informed About Sales Tax Trends:** Be aware of the evolving sales tax landscape, including economic nexus and marketplace facilitator laws, retail delivery and bag fees, and changes in sales tax holidays.

- **Plan for Pass-Through and Corporate Taxes:** Understanding the SALT cap is crucial for small business owners, especially with pass-through entities in high-tax states. Since 2020, this $10,000 cap can heighten your tax burden, limiting state and local tax deductions (*How Will Potential Changes in SALT Affect Tax Planning?* n.d.). A lifted or increased cap could reduce tax liabilities, fostering growth, while a maintained or lowered cap might hinder investments. Stay informed about upcoming changes to navigate these financial landscapes effectively. Also, be aware of the tax benefits set to expire in 2027 for pass-through and corporate entities.

- **Leverage First-Year Bonus Depreciation:** If applicable, use the first-year bonus depreciation to write off the cost of assets, such as vehicles and equipment, in one shot.

By staying ahead of these changes and seeking professional advice, you can navigate the new tax landscape effectively, ensuring your small business thrives in 2024. Remember, taxes are not just a compliance issue but also a strategic tool that, when managed well, can significantly impact your business's bottom line.

Overcoming Objections and Hesitations

Overcoming objections and hesitations about tax laws for small business owners involves a mix of awareness, strategic planning, and proactive action. As a small business owner, staying informed about evolving tax regulations and how they might impact your business is crucial. For instance, the expiring provisions of the Tax Cuts and Jobs Act, particularly the 199A pass-through deduction, are significant areas of concern for 2024 and beyond (Donaldson, 2023).

Understanding the IRS improvements and available tax credits and deductions is essential. Familiarize yourself with credits, such as the Clean Energy and Vehicle credits or the Small Business Health Care Tax Credit, which can offer substantial savings (Upcoming IRS Improvements, 2023). Additionally, strategic tax planning, such as leveraging retirement contributions and health savings accounts, can provide significant deductions, reducing your overall tax liability.

However, it's not just about understanding these possibilities but effectively using them. Many small business owners hesitate to adopt aggressive tax mitigation strategies due to perceived complexity or fear of audits. Yet, the potential savings often justify the risks involved. You should consider and implement strategies, such as entity structuring, pre-tax expenditures, generating tax-free income, and wealth accumulation when they fit your situation.

To effectively navigate these complexities, it's advisable to collaborate with a knowledgeable CPA, who can customize these strategies to your business requirements, ensuring compliance and maximizing benefits.

As a small business owner, understanding tax laws can be challenging, but several resources translate complex tax laws into easy-to-understand language:

- **Squire (squire.com)** offers comprehensive insights into tax changes affecting small businesses, including the impact of new laws and the role of certified public accountants in ensuring compliance. They highlight vital modifications in tax codes, such as net operating rules, interest expense limitations, and changes in charitable contribution limits, which are essential for small businesses to understand.

- **Block Advisors (blockadvisors.com)** explains tax law changes pertinent to small business owners. Their guide covers essential topics, such as PPP tax reporting, EIDL Advance loan reporting, and changes in business meal deductions. They also discuss self-employed sick leave, reporting changes, and business interest expense rate changes, which are crucial for effective tax planning.

- **PaySimple (paysimple.com)** offers guidance on essential tax laws for small businesses. Their resources include information on when to pay taxes, inventory deductions, home office expenses, entertainment expenses, and the Qualified Business Income Deduction. They also explain bonus depreciation, the Section 179 deduction, the cash method of accounting, the timing of retirement contributions, and the acceleration of expenses, all of which are vital for small business tax planning.

These websites provide valuable, user-friendly information, helping small business owners navigate the complexities of tax laws and make informed business decisions.

Remember, tax planning is a continuous process, and staying informed and proactive is vital to overcoming hesitations and objections regarding tax laws.

Key Takeaways

- Tax laws are complex and ever-changing, making it vital for small businesses to stay informed and adapt for compliance and strategic benefits.

- Failing to comply with tax laws can result in penalties, missed deductions, and higher effective tax rates, negatively impacting small businesses financially.

- Reliable resources for tax updates include the IRS Tax Reform Small Business Initiative, Small Business and Self-Employed Tax Center, and IRS tools and resources.

- To make the most of new tax laws, understand changes, maximize deductions and credits, adapt to reporting thresholds, and consult with tax professionals.

- Overcoming objections to tax laws requires awareness, strategic planning, and proactive action, emphasizing understanding of IRS improvements, tax credits, and deductions.

Having navigated the complexities of the ever-changing tax landscape, you understand the importance of staying updated and leveraging new laws. Now, let's focus on why tax planning isn't just a year-end scramble but a continuous, year-round activity essential for maximizing your business's financial health and potential.

STRATEGY 13 - MASTER YEAR-ROUND TAX VIGILANCE

"To master taxes, don't follow the calendar. Let every day be a step towards tax efficiency.

Planning for Taxes Year-Round

Due to the evolving financial environment, it's essential to recognize that tax planning is more than a year-end task, providing a year-round strategic advantage. Picture the tranquility of knowing you've maximized your tax situation at every opportunity, allowing you to reinvest every saved dollar into your business.

This chapter explores the perks of year-round tax planning, empowering you with actionable insights on seamlessly incorporating tax planning into your business activities. Discover the indispensable tools, resources, tips, and strategies that will redefine how you approach your taxes, making them a catalyst for your business's growth and prosperity.

The Perks of Year-Round Tax Planning

Proactively staying ahead in your financial endeavors as an entrepreneur is a key game changer. Year-round tax planning is an essential strategy that can significantly impact your business's economic health. Unlike the last-minute rush during tax season, a year-round approach ensures you're always prepared, maximizing opportunities and minimizing liabilities.

Maintaining regular records of your earnings and expenditures will give you a transparent understanding of your upcoming tax obligations, allowing you to strategize effectively.

Staying Ahead Of Tax Law Changes

Tax laws are dynamic, often evolving with economic and political shifts. For example, the U.S. corporate income tax rate remains at 21% in 2024, but there were talks of increasing it to 28% (Verbeck, 2023). Remaining well-informed about these changes empowers you to make decisions with awareness and knowledge. Regularly consulting with a tax professional can keep you updated on the latest tax regulations, credits, and deductions that affect your business.

Maximizing Tax Deductions And Credits

Continuous tax planning offers a significant advantage in optimizing deductions and credits. For example, pass-through businesses can claim the Qualified Business Income (QBI) deduction, enabling them to deduct as much as 20% of their income (Berry-Johnson, 2023). You can use the Section 179 deduction to subtract the entire cost of eligible equipment from your taxes (Verbeck, 2023). Planning year-round ensures you're taking full advantage of these deductions.

Improving Cash Flow Management

Tax planning plays a crucial role in effectively optimizing your cash flow. By spreading tax preparation throughout the year, you avoid the financial strain of year-end tax liabilities. This approach allows for better budgeting and economic forecasting, which is crucial for your business's smooth operation and growth.

Avoiding Penalties And Errors

Rushed tax preparations are prone to errors, leading to audits and penalties. A year-round approach reduces this risk, giving you ample time to cross-check and ensure accuracy in your tax filings. Starting early in the year to implement tax strategies is a prudent move.

Tailoring Strategies To Business Needs

Tax planning is not a one-size-fits-all solution because every business is distinct. It involves an ongoing process that enables you to customize strategies based on your business's size, industry, and specific activities. For instance, consider if you run your business as a sole proprietorship or an LLC. In that case, your business's taxes are automatically reflected in your taxes, necessitating a different planning approach than corporations.

Retirement And Benefit Planning

Offering retirement and benefits plans not only aids in employee retention but can also provide tax advantages. By reviewing your options regularly, you ensure you're maximizing the tax benefits of these plans.

Taking Advantage Of Tax Credits

Small businesses can access several tax credits, such as the Work Opportunity Tax Credit (WOTC) and the Disabled Access Credit (DAC). These often tie to specific actions or expenses and can directly reduce the taxes you owe.

Year-round tax planning is more than just a strategy. It's fundamental to running a successful business. By staying informed, maximizing deductions and credits, managing cash flow, avoiding penalties, tailoring strategy to your business, planning for retirement and employee benefits, and leveraging tax credits, you position your business for financial stability and growth.

How to Incorporate Tax Planning Into Your Business Activities

Incorporating tax planning into your small business activities is a crucial financial management and sustainability strategy. The dynamic tax landscape, highlighted by the 2024 Tax Reform, demands agility and informed decision-making to optimize tax benefits while complying with the law. Here's a comprehensive overview of integrating tax planning into your business operations, emphasizing its relevance to small businesses.

Understanding The Basics And Adjustments Required By Tax Reforms

To embark on your tax planning journey, you should understand the fundamental regulations governing income tax rates and deductions. Various forms of income undergo distinct taxation treatments, with ordinary income encompassing earnings, such as salaries, bonuses, self-employment income, and pass-through business earnings, representing the most prevalent category. Investment income, such as rents, royalties, and interest, are also taxed as ordinary income. At the same time, qualified dividends and long-term capital gains from assets held for more than one year are subject to special lower rates (*Tax Planning for Business Owners*, 2023).

The 2024 Tax Reform, a significant overhaul of the U.S. tax code, introduces changes that affect small businesses, necessitating adjustments in your tax planning strategies. Fundamental changes include a corporate tax rate reduction and a 20% deduction for pass-through entities (*How Does the 2024 Tax Reform Affect Year-End Tax Planning?* n.d.). However, the reform also limits certain deductions and credits, requiring a reevaluation of tax strategies.

Capital Expenditures And Depreciation

Small businesses rely on capital expenditures and depreciation as essential in their tax planning strategies. The 2024 Tax Reform impacts these areas significantly. The reform raises the limit on assets a business can expense under Section 179 to $1 million and extends the 100% bonus depreciation through 2024 (*How Does the 2024 Tax Reform Affect Year-End Tax Planning?* n.d.). These provisions enable businesses to deduct the expenses associated with specific capital assets during the year they are acquired, accelerating the reduction of taxable income.

Entity Choice And Structure

The 2024 Tax Reform significantly impacts the selection of business structures and entities for tax purposes. Transitioning from a tiered to a flat corporate tax rate and introducing a limit on the business income eligible for the lower pass-through tax rate play a crucial role. These alterations necessitate small businesses to reevaluate their choice of entity and structure for tax purposes, which could result in a change in business structure based on individual situations.

Practical Strategies For Small Businesses

- **Timing Income and Expenses:** Control the timing of recognizing income and accelerating deductions. This could include deferring income, such as consulting or self-employment, and advancing expenses, such as mortgage or charitable contributions.

- **Leveraging Retirement Incentives:** Utilize tax-efficient retirement incentives. Making required minimum distributions from retirement accounts and using your annual gift tax exclusion can contribute to tax savings.

- **Capitalizing on Deductions and Credits:** Small businesses need to refine their spending habits and adapt their tax planning strategies to take advantage of the increased deductions for business-related expenses and the restrictions on interest expense deductions.

- **Consulting With Tax Professionals:** Consulting with a professional tax advisor is crucial due to the complexity of tax laws and their ever-changing nature. They provide tailored advice and ensure strict compliance with the latest tax regulations.

Tax planning isn't something you do only at the end of the year. It's an ongoing integral part of your business operations. It involves staying updated, adjusting to developments like the 2024 Tax Reform, and strategically aligning your decisions with your business goals and tax responsibilities. Small businesses can boost their competitiveness, maintain financial stability, and lay the foundation for sustainable expansion.

Tools and Resources for Year-Round Tax Planning

As a small business owner, controlling your tax planning remains essential for your financial well-being. Here, we provide a customized guide to the tools and resources to support your year-round tax planning efforts.

- **Tax Planning Software:** TaxAct and TurboTax are excellent for estimating annual tax liabilities. They offer complete filing capabilities for different business structures, discount notifications, refund guarantees, and audit support.

- **Tax Calculators and Tools:** Platforms such as eFile.com offer tax estimation calculators, expert advice personalized to individual needs, and complimentary audit assistance. Platforms such as TripLog are great for tracking work-related travel expenses, including mileage, toll fares, parking fees, lodging, and meals.

- **IRS and Government Resources:** The Small Business and Self-Employed Tax Center provides an extensive collection of business forms, tax provisions, and additional resources, aiding in reducing the burden associated with preparing tax files and paperwork. The Directory of Federal Tax Return Preparers is another valuable resource for locating qualified tax return preparers.

- **Books and Educational Resources:** To enhance your tax preparation skills, consider investing in reputable tools, such as the *Thomson Reuters 1040 Quickfinder Handbook*, which offers comprehensive and user-friendly references. Platforms like Udemy and Coursera also provide courses that can deepen your understanding of small business taxes.

- **Accounting Software**: Using business accounting software, such as Intuit QuickBooks Online, Oracle NetSuite, FreshBooks, and Zoho Books, can automate accounting tasks and help keep financial documents organized, which is beneficial come tax season.

Tax planning requires continuous attention rather than being a task reserved solely for year-end activities. Using these tools and resources, you can actively plan, reduce tax liabilities, and avoid unexpected tax issues. Don't hesitate to contact experts and make the most of available technology and information. This proactive stance will set your business up for financial prosperity and expansion.

Tips and Strategies for Successful Tax Planning

As a small business owner, it's crucial to have mapped-out strategies for successful year-round tax planning. Here are key strategies:

- **Timing and Shifting Income and Expenses:** This strategy involves timing the recognition of income and shifting expenses to optimize taxable earnings. For instance, defer income to a later tax year or accelerate costs within the current year to reduce taxable income.

- **Utilizing Business Tax Deductions:** Deductions are vital in lowering your taxable income. Take, for instance, the Section 179 deduction that permits businesses to subtract the entire cost of eligible equipment and software purchases, encouraging investments in capital assets. The Qualified Business Income deduction also enables specific businesses to deduct as much as 20% of their qualified business income (Verbeck, 2023).

- **Maximizing Business Tax Credits and Incentives:** Tax credits actively decrease tax liability. Credits such as the Employee Retention Credit and Paid Family Leave Credit offer substantial tax benefits to businesses that fulfill specific requirements.

- **Optimizing Your Business Entity Structure:** Selecting the proper business structure, such as a sole proprietorship, LLC, or S corporation, has a substantial impact on your tax responsibilities. Opting for pass-through entities can lead to potential tax savings, allowing the company's net income to flow to the owner's tax return.

- **Strategizing International Operations:** Understanding cross-border tax laws and treaties is vital for businesses with global operations. Employing international tax planning strategies can minimize overall tax liability and mitigate potential double taxation.

- **Improving Tax Knowledge:** Staying informed about tax laws and regulations helps you make better financial decisions and remain compliant, thus avoiding penalties and maximizing potential savings.

- **Keeping Good Business Records:** Accurate recordkeeping is essential for documenting deductions, credits, and tax positions, which aids in effective tax planning and compliance.

- **Working With Tax Professionals:** Tax professionals possess expertise in intricate tax issues, aiding you in maintaining compliance while reducing tax liabilities. They can assist you in navigating diverse tax strategies and guarantee that you capitalize on all relevant tax advantages.

- **Leveraging Retirement Plan Contributions:** By encouraging retirement planning and facilitating tax savings, businesses and employees can reduce taxable income by maximizing contributions to retirement plans such as 401(k)s and IRAs.

- **Utilizing Accountable Plans for Employee Reimbursements:** Accountable plans for reimbursing employee expenses ensure that these costs are not classified as taxable income, reducing the business's payroll tax liabilities.

- **Taking Advantage of Tax Status Changes:** To determine if changing your tax status, such as opting for corporate taxation, can lead to tax savings, it's essential to collaborate with a professional who can assess its suitability for your business requirements and tax circumstances.

- **Implementing Efficient Business Systems:** Choosing the correct accounting, inventory, and payroll systems can improve operational efficiency, ensure accurate financial reporting, and maintain compliance with tax regulations.

Active participation in strategic tax planning is essential for minimizing liabilities and optimizing savings. Implementing these strategies can enhance your business's financial efficiency and compliance. However, due to the complexity of tax laws, consulting with qualified professionals is crucial to ensure proper implementation and compliance.

Key Takeaways

- Small businesses must engage in year-round tax planning to remain well-prepared, capitalize on opportunities, and minimize liabilities.

- Continuous tax planning optimizes deductions and credits, such as the Qualified Business Income deduction and Section 179 deduction.

- Effective tax planning improves cash flow management by spreading tax preparation throughout the year.

- A year-round approach reduces errors and the risk of penalties in tax filings.

- Incorporating tax planning into business activities involves understanding basics, adjusting to tax reforms, and aligning decisions with tax responsibilities.

- Tools, such as TaxAct, TurboTax, and IRS resources, assist in ongoing tax management.

- Strategies for successful tax planning include timing income and expenses, maximizing deductions and credits, and optimizing business entity structure.

You already explored effective tax planning as crucial for small businesses. Let's cut through the clutter with our Small Business Tax FAQ. In the next chapter, you'll find clear, concise answers to your pressing tax questions, empowering you to make informed decisions throughout the year.

STRATEGY 14-ANSWER TO SOME TAX MYSTERIES

"The only bad tax question is the one not asked. Inquire, learn, and leverage.

Tackling Common Tax Questions and Concerns

Given the constantly changing landscape of tax laws and regulations, small business owners may find the intricate realm of taxes overwhelming. The evolving nature of these regulations can lead to feelings of being buried in paperwork, but there's no need to worry! In this journey, you can maximize your tax deductions, choose the proper legal structure, and ensure your online business is tax-compliant.

From handling payroll and employee benefits to understanding the implications of having employees in different states, you'll find the guidance you need to thrive. It's not merely a matter of cutting through the clutter. Instead, it involves empowering yourself with knowledge, making informed decisions, and attaining financial success for your small business.

What Are the Most Important Tax Laws for Small Businesses?

For an entrepreneur, keeping up with the most pertinent tax laws is vital to ensure success. Consider these essential points to stay informed:

- **Increased Standard Deductions:** For tax year 2024, there's an uptick in standard deductions. Single filers can now claim $13,600, while married couples jointly filing can claim $27,200 (*3 Tax Changes for Small Businesses*, 2024). This change provides some relief by reducing taxable income.

- **Revised Mileage Rates:** The IRS now sets the standard mileage rate at 58 cents per mile for business-related transportation, an essential update for those who use their vehicles for business purposes (*3 Tax Changes for Small Businesses*, 2024).

- **Employer Tax Credits:** New tax credits are available for employers, providing benefits, such as paid family and medical leave, adoption assistance, or educational assistance. Check your eligibility to take advantage of these savings.

- **Proposed Corporate Tax Rate Increase:** There's a suggested increase in corporate tax rates from 21% to

28% in 2024 (*2024 Business Tax Law*, n.d.). This change could significantly impact your business's bottom line if it comes into effect.

- **Enhanced Deductions and Credits:** The Solar Investment Tax Credit has increased by 30% for solar projects to commence construction before 2025. Also, the R&D Tax Credit has become more accessible, allowing businesses to offset up to $250,000 of their payroll taxes (*2024 Business Tax Law*, n.d.).

- **Excess Business-Loss Limitation Rules:** Joint filers can now deduct losses up to a maximum of $540,000 annually, while single filers have a deduction cap of $270,000 (Herigstad, 2023). This change impacts how you can offset business income and losses.

- **Interest Expense Limitation Rule:** The limit on deductible interest expense includes business interest income, 30% of the adjusted taxable income, and interest expense from floor plan financing (Herigstad, 2023). This rule is vital for businesses with significant financing costs.

- **State and Local Tax (SALT) Cap:** Since 2020, filers can only deduct up to $10,000 in state and local taxes (Herigstad, 2023). This cap can significantly affect small businesses operating in high-tax states.

- **Tax Benefits for Pass-Through Entities and Corporations:** Pass-through businesses get a 20% deduction, phasing out at certain income levels. C corporations enjoy a lowered tax rate of 21% (Herigstad, 2023).

- **First-Year Bonus Depreciation:** Businesses can deduct the entire purchase cost of eligible equipment and property, which will be reduced annually in 2023 (Herigstad, 2023).

- **Sales Tax Laws:** As a small business owner, you must understand that sales tax laws vary by state and locality. Ensure compliance by registering in each state where you have nexus, collecting the correct sales tax rates, and filing returns on time.

- **Payroll Taxes:** As an entrepreneur, you must understand payroll tax laws. For instance, you must deduct Social Security and Medicare taxes from your employee's wages. These taxes, collectively known as FICA, are your responsibility to calculate, withhold, and remit to the IRS promptly, ensuring compliance and avoiding penalties.

Each decision can have significant tax implications. So, staying updated and proactive is vital to optimizing your financial outcomes.

How Can I Maximize My Tax Deductions as a Small Business Owner?

Maximizing tax deductions is crucial for financial success. Here's how you can do it effectively:

- **Maintain Impeccable Records:** Diligently maintain all receipts, invoices, and relevant documents for your business expenses. This practice is crucial for precise tax filing and serves as necessary proof in the event of an audit.

- **Understand and Utilize Available Deductions:** Various deductions are available to small businesses, including:

- **Travel Expenses:** You can fully deduct business-related expenses, such as transportation, hotels, flights, and meals, for business purposes.

- **Business Meals:** Deduct 50% of meal expenses with business contacts and 100% during business travel (Standberry, n.d.).

- **Salaries and Wages:** Deduct salaries, wages, bonuses, commissions, and employer-paid benefits.

- **Depreciation:** Account for the wear and tear of assets over time, using methods such as Section 179 Deduction.

- **Education Expenses:** Deduct costs related to workshops, seminars, and training that enhance business skills.

- **Professional Fees:** Legal, accounting, consultation, and marketing fees are deductible.

- **Stay Informed on Tax Law Changes:** Stay informed about changes in tax laws by regularly updating yourself on new guidelines and regulations at the federal, state, and local levels.

- **Leverage Section 179:** This effective tool subtracts the entire expense of eligible equipment and property in the year they are acquired.

- **Optimize Employee Benefits:** You can deduct contributions to retirement plans and health savings accounts (HSAs), offering tax benefits.

- **Explore Home Office Deductions:** You qualify for a home office deduction by dedicating a section of your house exclusively to business purposes.

- **Plan for Depreciation:** Grasp how to schedule asset depreciation and leverage the tax benefits it offers.

- **Hire a Tax Professional:** To take advantage of credits and deductions, actively engage with a qualified tax professional. They can help ensure you maximize all options.

Stay informed, utilize available deductions, and optimize your financial strategies to reduce tax liability and retain more money in your business.

Which Legal Structure Is Best for My Business From a Tax Perspective?

Choosing the proper legal structure for your business is crucial, not only for operational purposes but also for optimizing your tax situation. Let's delve into the famous business structures and understand their tax implications, guiding you to make a well-informed decision.

- **Sole Proprietorship:** The simplest business entity provides no legal separation between the owner and the business. It's straightforward to set up and manage, but it does come with personal liability for business debts and obligations. From a tax perspective, sole proprietorships are "pass-through" entities, meaning the business pays no taxes. Instead, the owner's tax return absorbs the profits and losses. However, this also entails paying self-employment tax on all your earnings.

- **Partnership:** In a partnership, two or more individuals collectively own and actively engage in all facets of the business, sharing both profits and losses. Although partnerships file tax returns to disclose income, deductions, gains, and losses, they do not face income tax at the entity level. Instead, each partner reports their profits and losses on their tax returns. Partnerships are particularly advantageous for businesses with multiple owners and professional groups, such as lawyers and accountants.

- **Limited Liability Company (LLC):** They offer a blend of corporate liability protection and the tax advantages seen in sole proprietorships or partnerships. LLC owners benefit from safeguarding their assets against business debts. Regarding taxes, LLCs follow pass-through taxation, meaning the business's earnings are reported on the owners' tax returns, sidestepping the dual taxation encountered by C Corporations.

- **Corporations (C and S):**

    C Corporation: A C corporation is distinct from its owners in a legal sense and provides essential protection against personal liability. Nonetheless, it encounters the challenge of dual taxation. The corporate entity itself is subject to taxes, and shareholders must report and pay taxes on dividends in their tax filings. Big businesses frequently prefer C corporations, as they can generate capital by selling company stocks.

    S Corporation: An S corporation, also known as an S Corp, operates with pass-through taxation akin to LLCs. It's a viable option for small businesses that meet specific

IRS criteria. It allows profits and certain losses to flow directly into the owners' income, avoiding corporate tax rates.

Each legal structure has distinct advantages and disadvantages. A sole proprietorship or partnership might suit businesses with lower risks and simpler operations. In contrast, LLCs offer a balance of liability protection and tax simplicity, which is ideal for many small to medium-sized businesses. A C corporation could be the best fit for larger companies or those seeking to raise capital through the sale of stock.

Base your decision on the particular needs of your business and its growth plans. You should seek advice from a legal or tax expert to understand how each structure aligns with your business objectives and tax planning. Remember, the best choice varies based on individual circumstances, and what's best for one business might not suit another.

How Do I Handle Payroll, Employee Benefits, and Compensation for Tax Purposes?

Handling payroll, employee benefits, and compensation for tax purposes requires staying informed and adaptable. Here's a brief guide to help you remain on the correct path:

- **Stay Updated With Social Security and Medicare Changes:** In 2024, the Social Security wage base limit will increase to $168,600, with the tax rate at 6.2% for employers and employees. For Medicare, the tax rate remains 1.45% for each, but remember, there's an additional 0.9% Medicare tax on wages exceeding $200,000 (*2024 Federal Payroll Tax Rates*, n.d.).

- **Adhere to Federal Income Tax Bracket Adjustments:** The IRS revises tax brackets yearly. In 2024, these adjustments reflect ongoing inflation, potentially reducing employee payroll tax burdens across various income brackets.

- **Understand the Tax Relief for American Families and Workers Act of 2024:** This act introduces several changes, including enhanced child tax credits and support for small businesses to alleviate economic pressures and promote growth.

- **Monitor Changes in 401(k) and SIMPLE Plan Limits:** The maximum employee pretax contribution for 401(k) plans increases to $23,000, and the SIMPLE plan limit to $16,000 (*2024 Federal Payroll Tax Rates*, n.d.).

- **Ensure Compliance With New Hire Reporting Requirements:** Employers must report basic information about new or returning employees within a specific time frame to avoid penalties.

- **Use the Electronic Federal Tax Payment System (EFTPS) for Tax Liabilities:** Employers should use the EFTPS for federal tax liabilities unless their quarterly payroll tax liabilities are less than $2,500 (*2024 Federal Payroll Tax Rates*, n.d.).

- **File W-2 and 1099 Forms Timely:** Make sure to meet the deadlines for submitting these forms on time. The due date for filing 2023 Form W-2 is January 31, 2024. The same deadline applies for Form 1099-NEC (*2024 Federal Payroll Tax Rates*, n.d.).

- **Include Health Benefits on W-2 Reporting:** Employers must disclose the total cost of health benefits provided by the employer on W-2 forms.

- **Be Mindful of Household Employment Tax Requirements:** For domestic workers paid cash wages of

$2,700 or more in 2024, employers must withhold and pay FICA taxes (*2024 Federal Payroll Tax Rates*, n.d.).

It is essential to be proactive and thorough in managing payroll, employee benefits, and compensation for tax purposes. This ensures compliance, avoids penalties, and benefits the employer and employee long-term.

How Do I Keep Up With Changes in Tax Laws and Regulations?

For small business owners, staying updated on tax laws and regulatory shifts is vital to maintain compliance and maximize potential tax benefits. Here are essential suggestions to keep you informed about these updates:

- **Utilize Professional Services:** Connect with tax experts or accounting firms specializing in small business taxes. These professionals offer tailored guidance and ensure you stay informed about any pertinent updates in the field.

- **Regularly Visit Government Websites:** Bookmark and visit websites of relevant tax authorities, such as the IRS. These websites often have sections dedicated to updates and guidance for small businesses.

- **Subscribe to Newsletters:** Subscribe to newsletters and alerts from websites and professional service firms specializing in tax matters. These sources regularly offer brief updates on significant changes in tax regulations.

- **Attend Workshops and Seminars:** Participate in tax workshops, webinars, or seminars hosted by tax professionals or business associations. These events can offer valuable insights into recent tax changes and their implications.

- **Join Business Associations:** Joining local or national business associations is beneficial, as they frequently furnish their members with valuable information on tax modifications and other regulatory revisions.

- **Stay Updated with Business News:** Regularly read business news, especially sections focusing on finance and taxation. They often cover significant changes in tax laws and their impact on businesses.

- **Use Tax Software:** You should utilize regularly updated tax software to maintain compliance and stay informed about new tax responsibilities. This approach can help you meet your tax obligations and comprehend any newly introduced tax laws.

- **Network:** Connect with fellow business owners through networking groups or online forums. Collaborating and exchanging experiences and expertise with peers can offer valuable, real-world insights into navigating tax reforms and adjustments.

- **Leverage Social Media:** Follow tax experts and relevant government bodies on social media platforms. They often share updates and insights on tax changes.

Staying proactive and well-informed about tax laws is crucial for effective financial planning and avoiding any compliance issues.

How Do I Manage the Taxes for My Online Company?

Managing taxes for your online business may appear challenging, but with the appropriate approach, you can handle it. First, keep track of your tax deadlines. For e-commerce businesses, key dates include:

- partnership and S corp tax filing (March 15)
- personal and corporate tax filing (April 18)
- quarterly estimated tax payments (April 18, June 15, September 15, and January 16)

Missing these deadlines can lead to penalties, so mark them in your calendar (*How to Prepare Taxes*, 2023).

Organize your bookkeeping and records thoroughly. This includes reviewing all potential e-commerce tax deductions, such as home office, education, internet and phone, web hosting, online service fees, equipment, shipping costs, vehicle use, contract labor costs, and professional services. Ensuring accurate and comprehensive records will allow you to maximize these deductions.

Moreover, understand your sales tax obligations. The U.S. Supreme Court's South Dakota v. Way fair ruling means e-commerce retailers must pay sales tax, which varies by state

(*Sales Tax 101 for Online Sellers*, 2023). When your business creates a physical presence or nexus in a state, the standard obligation involves actively collecting sales tax in that particular state.

As an online business owner, navigating sales tax complexities is essential. The concept of "nexus" determines your sales tax duties. For example, if you run an Etsy store from Nevada, you must charge sales tax to Nevada buyers.

Additionally, you might have to collect sales tax in other states where you have a nexus. The tax treatment for digital goods and services often differs from physical items. Therefore, as an online course creator, it's essential to understand the specific tax regulations for your digital products across various states and countries, ensuring compliance and avoiding legal complications.

Consider working with a qualified tax professional, especially one experienced in e-commerce. A professional can offer personalized advice for your specific business and industry, aiding you in navigating intricate tax regulations and pinpointing relevant deductions. Additionally, they can guarantee compliance with all regulatory obligations, preventing expensive errors.

Finally, stay informed about tax changes and updates relevant to online businesses. Utilize resources, such as Gusto, for insights into tax deductions specific to online selling, including materials, labor, inventory, educational expenses, home internet, and office expenses. Taking proactive steps and consulting with experts can streamline the tax season, reducing stress and enhancing efficiency for your online business.

What Are the Tax Consequences of Employing Workers in Different States?

When you employ staff in different states, you navigate a complex tax landscape. Each state has unique tax rules that impact income and corporate taxes. For instance, you may face dual income tax filings if your employees work remotely across state lines. Employers must often comply with taxes in multiple jurisdictions, creating a "tax nexus" where business operations in a state trigger tax liabilities. This situation can become intricate, particularly with remote workers in several states.

States such as New York, Pennsylvania, and Kansas, where dual residency is typical, exemplify the challenges. If you or your employees live part-time in different states, managing income tax obligations in both can lead to hefty bills. The general rule is that if you spend 183 or more days in a state, you're considered a resident for tax purposes and must pay total income tax on all annual income (Rosenberg, 2023). Moreover, changing your state of residency for tax purposes isn't automatic and requires satisfying various conditions, such as voter and vehicle registration and driver's licenses.

Remote work arrangements also impact sales, use, and business personal property taxes. Even a remote worker might change your business's tax obligations, particularly for smaller businesses. Local taxes, often mirroring state levies, can also be triggered by remote employees. Companies with remote employees working outside the state where they initially received state and local tax credits and incentives must reassess their eligibility for these benefits.

Therefore, staying informed and seeking professional tax advice is vital to navigating these complex scenarios effectively. With remote work becoming more prevalent, understanding these tax implications is crucial for ensuring compliance and optimizing your tax strategy.

What Are the Tax Implications of Operating My Business From Home?

As a home-based entrepreneur, you're eligible for various deductions, which can substantially boost your economic health. However, navigating these waters requires strategic planning and meticulous recordkeeping.

First and foremost, the IRS permits deductions for a segment of your home that you use solely for business purposes. You must designate this space for business activities. You can calculate through two methods: the standard approach, which entails determining the percentage of your home utilized for business, or the simplified method, which employs a fixed rate per square foot of business use.

Moreover, operating from home opens up the possibility of numerous deductions. These range from vehicle expenses used for business purposes, employee payments, retirement plans, rent, interest on business loans, business taxes, insurance, travel, supplies, materials, and professional services to marketing and business development costs.

Don't overlook the opportunity to employ family members, such as your children, as this can shift income into a lower tax bracket and offer additional deductions. Maintaining thorough documentation for meals during business meetings and travels is essential and often partially or fully deductible.

However, the intent to make a profit is crucial. You can't just start a home business to write off home expenses. The IRS requires proof of your profit motive, which includes maintaining sales records, having a business plan, using bookkeeping services, and creating a separate business bank account.

Running a business from home means navigating a landscape of complex tax deductions and regulations. By understanding and utilizing these deductions and keeping diligent records, you can maximize the financial benefits of your home-based business venture.

Key Takeaways

- Fundamental tax laws for small businesses include increased standard deductions, revised mileage rates, new employer tax credits, and proposed corporate tax rate increases.

- To maximize tax deductions, maintain accurate records, leverage available deductions, such as travel and meal expenses, and stay informed on tax law changes.

- Choosing the proper legal structure (sole proprietorship, partnership, LLC, C corporation, or S corporation) impacts tax implications and liability protections.

- Handle payroll and employee benefits by adhering to updated tax brackets, utilizing EFTPS for tax liabilities, and complying with reporting requirements for W-2 and 1099 forms.

- Stay updated with tax laws by engaging with tax professionals, attending workshops, subscribing to newsletters, and regularly visiting government websites.

- For online businesses, track tax deadlines, organize bookkeeping, understand sales tax obligations, work with a tax professional, and stay informed about e-commerce tax changes.

- Having employees in different states creates complex tax situations due to varying state tax laws, requiring compliance with multiple jurisdictions.

- Operating a business from home allows for deductions, such as a home office, vehicle expenses, and employee payments, but requires proof of profit intent and accurate recordkeeping.

Navigating the intricate realm of small business taxation may seem daunting. However, as you delve into the essentials of tax laws, excel in deductions, and address the intricacies of payroll and taxes for employees in different states, the next chapter equips you to handle your business's tax responsibilities confidently.

STRATEGY 15-LEAP OVER TAX OBSTACLES

"Tax hurdles are not blockades but stepping stones to greater financial acumen.

How to overcome Tax Hurdles

As an entrepreneur, the complexities of tax season are all too familiar to you. This guide specifically caters to your needs, tackling pressing tax issues head-on. We explore common challenges, offer practical solutions, and provide clear, direct responses to your tax-related queries.

Whether deciphering complex tax codes or strategizing to maximize deductions, this guide is your ally. We understand your unique tax hurdles and offer supportive, authoritative advice to navigate these challenges confidently. Empower yourself with knowledge and strategies that make tax season less daunting and more manageable.

Understanding Your Concerns: Addressing Common Tax Objections

As a small business owner, you must understand and navigate the complex tax landscape to avoid pitfalls that could lead to significant penalties and impede your business's growth. Be aware of these critical tax issues that demand your attention:

- **Underestimating the Importance of Accurate Record Keeping:** As a small business owner, you must keep your records current and comprehensive. Ensure you meticulously track all your business expenses, particularly those eligible for deductions, such as meals, entertainment, and vehicle expenses. If the IRS audits you and finds inadequate documentation, you risk losing these deductions, which could lead to higher tax bills and possible penalties.

- **Misunderstanding Deductions and Credits:** Small businesses have various deductions and credits available, such as the Qualified Business Income Deduction, Section 179 deduction, and deductions for energy-efficient commercial buildings. Misinterpreting these can lead to missed opportunities to reduce tax liabilities or over-claiming, which could flag an IRS audit.

- **Overlooking Quarterly Estimated Tax Payments:** If

your business expects a tax liability of $1,000 or more, making quarterly estimated tax payments is vital. Not adhering to this requirement can lead to penalties and accrual of interest. Calculate these payments accurately to avoid underpayment and overpayment (*Small Business Tax Issues*, 2021).

- **Misclassifying Employees and Contractors:** Incorrectly categorizing an individual as an independent contractor instead of an employee, or vice versa, can lead to tax fraud allegations. This misclassification affects payroll tax liabilities and can trigger an audit from the Employee Development Department.

- **Neglecting Self-Employment Taxes:** Being self-employed means you are accountable for the employer and employee portions of Social Security and Medicare taxes, totaling 15.3% of your net self-employment income. Neglecting to include this in your calculations can result in a surprisingly high tax liability (*Small Business Tax Issues*, 2021).

- **Failing to Report All Income, Including Cash Payments:** Cash-based businesses must maintain precise records of every transaction, as the IRS closely examines income reports. Any discrepancies can prompt audits and lead to the imposition of penalties.

- **Over-Deducting Business Expenses:** Small business owners often claim deductions for expenses, such as phone bills, home office use, and travel. It's crucial, however, to separate personal expenses from business expenses, as the IRS closely examines these deductions. Maintaining detailed records is critical to supporting these deduction claims effectively.

- **Ignoring State and Local Tax (SALT) Cap:** Since 2020, there's been a cap of $10,000 on deducting state and local taxes, which can significantly impact business owners in high-tax states (Herigstad, 2023). You need to understand the impact of this cap on your business for precise tax planning.

- **Underpaying Personal Income Tax:** Some business owners mistakenly believe that estimated quarterly tax payments are optional. However, these payments are mandatory, and failure to pay them on time and in full can lead to penalties, interest, and inflated end-of-year taxes.

Remember that tax laws are continually changing, and you must keep yourself informed and consult with experts to manage these changes effectively. This proactive stance guarantees that your business complies with the most recent tax regulations, preserving compliance and financial well-being.

Practical Solutions: Navigating Common Tax Pain Points

To effectively manage the common tax problems you're facing as a small business owner, consider these tailored solutions:

- **Keeping Accurate Record**s: Cultivate a rigorous approach to maintaining records. Use tax software or technological tools to systematically organize and monitor all business dealings, focusing on tracking deductible expenses, such as meals, entertainment, and vehicle costs. This practice not only eases the tax filing process but also strengthens your defense in case of an IRS audit.

- **Understanding Deductions and Credits:** Familiarize yourself with tax benefits available for your business, including the qualified business income deduction and the Section 179 deduction, to leverage them effectively. Being well-informed about these options can enhance your tax savings. Make sure to apply these deductions accurately and avoid claiming more than you're entitled to, as this could lead to IRS attention.

- **Managing Quarterly Estimated Tax Payments:** Establish a method for calculating and making your quarterly estimated tax payments, particularly if you anticipate owing more than $1,000 in taxes (*Small Business*

Tax Issues, 2021). This proactive approach helps avoid penalties and interest associated with underpayment or late payments.

- **Properly Classifying Employees and Contractors:** Ensure you clearly distinguish between employees and independent contractors to correctly impact payroll tax liabilities and prevent complications with tax authorities. If there's any uncertainty, consult a tax advisor or refer to IRS guidelines to classify them accurately.

- **Handling Self-Employment Taxes:** Self-employment necessitates covering the employee and employer portions of Social Security and Medicare taxes. This proactive stance ensures you avoid unexpected tax bills and comply with tax laws.

- **Reporting All Income:** Be diligent in reporting all income, including cash payments. Implement a robust bookkeeping system to accurately record all transactions and avoid discrepancies that might lead to IRS audits.

- **Discerning Business Expenses:** When claiming deductions for expenses, such as phone, home office, and travel, maintain detailed records to prove these are business-related. The IRS often scrutinizes mixed-use expenses, so clear documentation is vital.

- **Navigating the SALT Cap:** Stay aware of the $10,000 cap on state and local tax deductions, primarily if your business operates in a high-tax state (Herigstad, 2023). Accurate tax planning and avoiding unforeseen tax obligations rely on thoroughly grasping this concept.

- **Addressing Underpaid Personal Income Tax:** Viewing estimated quarterly tax payments as obligatory rather than optional is vital. Making these payments is crucial for preventing penalties and minimizing year-end tax liability. Employing reminders is a practical method to guarantee consistent adherence to these significant tax responsibilities.

Because tax laws and rules can change, it's vital to remain updated and confer with professionals when necessary. This proactive stance will enable you to effectively handle your tax responsibilities and concentrate on the growth of your business.

Answering Your Questions: Tackling Common Tax Queries

Here's a comprehensive FAQ for small business owners:

Should I Pay Taxes Annually Or Quarterly?

If your anticipated tax bill is under $1,000, you can pay it once a year. However, for a tax bill of $1,000 or more, it's advisable to opt for quarterly estimated payments to prevent any penalties due to underpayment (Moran, 2022).

What Counts As A Valid Tax Deduction For Businesses?

Ordinary expenses (typical within your industry) for operating your business can generally be deducted. These include office supplies, legal fees, and business education.

What's The Tax Filing Deadline?

You must file your federal income tax returns every year by April 15. However, if April 15 lands on a weekend or holiday, you should file your return on the next ordinary business day (*When to File*, n.d.).

Should I File A Tax Extension?

Consider filing an extension if you need more time for documentation, bookkeeping, or determining cash flow for retirement contributions. This gives an additional six months without a late filing penalty.

What If My Taxes Are Late?

Submit your tax filings promptly to prevent accruing additional penalties and interest. It's important to note that obtaining a filing extension doesn't grant extra time for making tax payments.

What Does An Irs Audit Mean For My Business?

When the IRS audits your tax return, they thoroughly investigate various areas, such as income, expenses, or claimed credits. During an audit, you must submit extra documentation to support the details of your return.

What Should I Do If I Owe A Balance To The Irs?

First, verify the amount you owe. You can pay in full, get a short-term payment plan (for balances under $100,000), or set up a long-term payment plan for amounts less than $25,000 (Moran, 2022).

Are Gym Memberships Deductible?

Generally, gym memberships are personal expenses and not deductible. However, the costs might be deductible if you have a private gym for employees at your business location.

Can I Deduct My Home Office?

You can claim a deduction for your home office if you use it solely and regularly for business activities. There are two ways to calculate this deduction: using a standard rate based on the office's square footage or calculating the actual expenses you've incurred.

What About Car Expenses For Business Use?

Ensure the car loan's name aligns with the account you use for payments. Appropriately claim deductions for business-related mileage and other car expenses.

Are Leasing Vehicles And Materials For Jobs Deductible?

Yes, leasing costs for vehicles and materials used for business are deductible.

Is It Possible To Deduct Expenses For Business Meals And Entertainment?

You can deduct 50% of your documented business meal expenses. However, since the Tax Cuts and Jobs Act of 2017–2018, entertainment expenses no longer qualify for deductions (Herigstad, 2023).

Is There a Maximum Deduction Limit for Gifts Given to Clients?

You can spend up to $25 on each gift per person, excluding

items that cost $4 or less, which don't count toward this limit (Herigstad, 2023).

Are Travel Expenses For Business Deductible?

Business-related travel expenses are deductible. However, for trips that serve both personal and business purposes, you can only deduct costs associated with the business aspect.

What About Work Clothing And Uniforms?

If the clothing is mandatory for your job and unsuitable for everyday wear, its cost and upkeep are deductible.

Can My Company Cover My Health Insurance Expenses?

Your business might qualify for the Small Business Health Care Tax Credit if it meets specific criteria.

Is The Life Insurance Premium Paid By Business Deductible?

Generally, life insurance premiums are not deductible if you, the business owner, are the beneficiary.

How Do I Handle Losses On Broken Equipment Or Vehicles?

If the asset is unusable, you should get rid of it and report a loss equivalent to its remaining depreciation. However, once you've expensed it under Section 179, this action doesn't allow for any more tax reductions through additional deductions.

Are Student Loan Interests Deductible On Business Returns?

While student loan interest isn't deductible separately on business returns, it can be part of an educational assistance program. You can deduct up to $2,500 on personal tax returns in student loan interest (Herigstad, 2023).

How Can I Establish An Effective Chart Of Accounts With Best Practices?

Use a numbering system with different ranges for different account types, such as assets, liabilities, equity, income, and expenses.

These answers provide a foundational understanding for small business owners navigating their tax responsibilities.

Key Takeaways

- Accurate recordkeeping is essential for tracking deductible business expenses and avoiding IRS penalties.

- Understanding available tax deductions and credits, such as the Qualified Business Income Deduction, can optimize tax savings.

- Small businesses must pay quarterly estimated taxes if they expect their tax liability to be over $1,000 to avoid penalties.

- Accurately categorizing workers as independent contractors or employees is critical to prevent misclassification penalties.

- Self-employed individuals must pay the employer's and employee's portions of Medicare and Social Security taxes.

- To prevent IRS audits and penalties, you should meticulously report every form of income, including cash transactions.

- Deducting business expenses requires careful distinction between personal and business use, with detailed records for IRS scrutiny.

- Businesses in states with higher taxes must consider the $10,000 limit on state and local tax deductions when planning their taxes.

- Estimated tax payments are mandatory, and underpaying can lead to penalties and increased end-of-year taxes.

- By continuously refreshing your understanding of tax laws and actively seeking guidance from tax professionals, you maintain your business's compliance and safeguard its financial well-being.

As a small business owner, maneuvering through the intricacies of taxation can be intricate, but rest assured you have a support system on this path. You are better prepared to approach tax obstacles confidently with the insights gained here. Let's transition to the conclusion, emphasizing the empowerment of your business's financial future.

CONCLUSION

As we turn the final page of *Small Business Tax Hacks*, you stand at the threshold of a new chapter in your entrepreneurial journey. Armed with a comprehensive understanding of the tax landscape and strategies to navigate it effectively, you're ready to transform the way you approach taxes—from a source of stress to a catalyst for growth and efficiency.

Reflecting on the Journey

We embarked on this journey together, starting with the basics of tax laws and regulations, laying a solid foundation for compliance and strategic planning. Through each chapter, we delved deeper into the complexities of the tax system, uncovering opportunities to minimize liabilities, maximize deductibles, and, ultimately, drive financial growth in your business.

- **From Basics to Strategy:** We began by grounding ourselves in the essential knowledge of tax laws to avoid common pitfalls and ensure compliance.

- **Maximizing Deductions:** We explored the nuances of tax deductions, learning how to identify and leverage opportunities to reduce our tax bills.

- **Strategic Structure and Bookkeeping:** We navigated the decisions surrounding business structures and the critical role of efficient bookkeeping, setting the stage for long-term success.

- **Advanced Tactics:** From handling payroll and benefits to mastering the intricacies of capital gains and depreciation, we armed ourselves with the tools needed for sophisticated tax planning and strategy.

Your Next Steps

With this knowledge at your fingertips, consider these actionable steps to begin applying what you've learned:

- **Evaluate Your Business Structure:** Reflect on the insights from Strategy 3 to determine if your current business structure aligns with your tax optimization goals.

- **Implement Efficient Bookkeeping Practices:** Use the techniques from Strategy 4 to streamline your financial recordkeeping, making tax time less daunting.

- **Explore a New Tax Credit:** Identify at least one new tax credit discussed in Strategy 9 that you haven't claimed before, and investigate how it can benefit your business this tax season.

Keep the Momentum Going

To ensure this book marks the beginning, not the end, of your tax optimization journey, I invite you to:

- **Join Our Community:** Visit www.firststellarhorizon.com to subscribe to our newsletter for the latest tax tips, updates, and success stories from fellow entrepreneurs.

- **Engage with Continuous Learning:** Follow our blog and attend webinars to stay informed about tax law changes and new strategies.

Looking Ahead

Your story of transformation is just beginning. With the strategies and insights from this guide, you're equipped to navigate the tax landscape with confidence and clarity. Remember, the journey from tax turmoil to triumph is not just about saving on taxes but about unlocking the full potential of your business. Here's to your success, and remember—you can do it!

Review Request Page
Free Goodwill

Hey there,

What a ride it's been, huh? You've been through the whole maze—ducking those pesky liabilities, grabbing every deductible in sight, boosting that ROI, and unlocking some serious growth for your biz. And now, with "Small Business Tax Hacks" as your secret weapon, you're the captain of your ship, charting a course straight for Success Island.

But wait, there's more to this story, and it's all about passing the baton. Imagine this: there are small business owners and bright-eyed entrepreneurs everywhere. They're out there right now, probably sipping on their third cup of coffee, trying to crack the code you've just mastered. What if you could be their Yoda?

Just by sharing your two cents about this book on Amazon, you're throwing them a lifeline. It's not just a review; it's like building a lighthouse for all those weary entrepreneurial travelers sailing through the night.

Here's how you can light up their journey:

Drop your thoughts here with a review on Amazon

https://www.amazon.com/review/review-your-purchases/?asin=B0CZSF1Z7K

Your words are more than just words; they're like a secret handshake to a new world of savvy tax moves. By dropping your review, you're not just being super helpful; you're keeping the magic of "Small Business Tax Hacks" alive and kicking.

Thanks a million for being more than a reader—you're a trailblazer, a mentor, a hero to someone who's probably out there hoping for a sign right now. This isn't just about tax hacks; it's about sparking a revolution of growth, smarts, and small business victories.
So here's to you and the waves of success you will set in motion.

TYLER HARRISON

You're awesome,

With heartfelt thanks,

Tyler Harrison & The First Stellar Horizon Team

GLOSSARY

401(k) and Pension Contributions Deduction: You can deduct contributions to retirement accounts such as SEP IRAs or solo 401(k)s.

Advertising and Marketing Deduction: You can deduct expenses for promoting your business, such as social media advertisements and business cards.

Affordable Care Act (ACA): A federal law requires businesses with at least 50 full-time employees to offer health insurance.

Bad Debts Deduction: You can deduct bad debts, including unpaid accounts receivable or loans issued by your business.

Balance Sheet: A financial statement that presents a momentary view of a company's financial status by detailing its assets, liabilities, and equity at a particular point in time.

Bonus Depreciation: An allowance enabling businesses to deduct a defined percentage of the expenses associated with eligible assets, influencing financial reporting and tax obligations.

Business-Loss Limitation Rules: These rules limit the amount of business losses for deduction in a tax year.

C Corporation: A business structure that offers strong asset protection and the ability to raise capital through stock sales but faces double taxation on profits.

Capital Gains Tax Rate: The taxation of capital gains depends on income levels and the duration of ownership, leading to varying tax rates.

Capital Gains: This term refers to the profit achieved by selling a capital asset, such as stocks, real estate, or a business, at a price higher than the initial purchase price.

Certified Public Accountant (CPA): This refers to a licensed accountant with expertise in accounting and tax laws.

Child Tax Credit: A credit that reduces the federal income tax owed by eligible parents for each qualifying child.

COBRA: The Consolidated Omnibus Budget Reconciliation Act permits employees to maintain their health insurance coverage after leaving a job.

Corporate Income Tax Rate: The term refers to the percentage of a corporation's income payable as taxes to the government.

Debt Interest and Loss Carryovers Deduction: You can deduct the interest you've paid on business debts and carry specific business losses to future tax years.

Depreciation: Spreading out the expense of assets such as vehicles and equipment for tax and financial purposes over their helpful lifespan.

Direct Home Office Expenses Deduction: 100% deductible expenses related directly to a home office, such as repairs and maintenance specific to the office area.

Disabled Access Credit: Businesses can claim a tax credit when they enhance their facilities to make them more accessible to individuals with disabilities.

Double Declining Balance: An accelerated depreciation method calculates higher depreciation expenses in the early years of an asset's life.

Double Taxation: This term refers to the taxation of profits at the corporate and shareholder levels for dividends in a corporation.

Dual Income Tax Filings: Employees working remotely across state lines can lead to dual income tax filings, where they must file tax returns in multiple states. Understanding the implications of dual income tax filings is crucial for compliance.

E-Filing Threshold: The number of tax returns a business must electronically file, which can impact accounting processes and investments.

Earned Income Tax Credit (EITC): A tax credit that provides financial support to individuals and families with low to moderate income and allows for refunds.

Employee Benefit Programs Deduction: You can deduct expenses associated with offering employee benefits, including health benefits, educational assistance, Flexible Spending Accounts (FSAs), and retirement plans.

Employee Retention Credit: A tax credit incentivizes businesses to retain employees, especially during challenging times. Understanding the eligibility criteria is essential for maximizing this credit.

Energy Investment Tax Credit (ITC): Companies that choose to invest in renewable energy sources such as solar panels and wind turbines are eligible for a tax credit.

Enrolled Agent (EA): This term describes a tax advisor recognized by the U.S. government as authorized to represent taxpayers before the IRS. EAs possess expertise in tax laws and can offer expert guidance.

Estimated Tax Payments: Quarterly payments made by self-employed individuals and businesses to cover their expected tax liability, helping avoid penalties.

Estimated Taxes: Businesses and self-employed individuals make quarterly tax payments to cover their expected tax liabilities. Timely and accurate estimation is vital to avoid penalties.

Fair Labor Standards Act (FLSA): This federal labor law regulates standards for wages and hours, including the provision for overtime pay.

Federal Income Tax: The portion of an employee's income

withheld by employers and remitted to the federal government to cover federal income tax obligations.

Federal Insurance Contributions Act (FICA): Under this law, employees and employers must pay Social Security and Medicare taxes.

Federal Unemployment Tax (FUTA): Employers contribute to a fund that covers unemployment benefits for eligible workers.

First-Year Bonus Depreciation: This provision enables businesses to deduct the entire cost of eligible equipment and property in the year they purchase, leading to potential tax savings.

Forms 941, 943, 944, 945, and 940: Federal forms used by employers for reporting and remitting payroll taxes to the IRS.

Gross Receipts: This term refers to a business's total revenue or income before any deductions.

Health Savings Account (HSA) Deduction: Deduction for contributions made to an HSA, with funds used for qualified health expenses being tax-free.

Home Office Deduction: A deduction that permits business owners to subtract expenses associated with a section of their home used solely for business activities.

Income Statement: This is a financial statement that provides an overview of a company's earnings, expenditures, and net income during a defined timeframe, usually spanning a month, quarter, or year.

Inflation Reduction Act: Legislation that affects various tax credits and deductions, often changing their limits and rules.

Interest Expense Limitation Rule: This rule limits the deductible interest expenses that businesses can claim, considering adjusted taxable income and other factors.

IRS Audit: An investigation by the Internal Revenue Service (IRS) into a taxpayer's financial records, including depreciation calculations.

IRS Free File Program: A service offering free tax filing options for individuals below certain income thresholds, ensuring accurate returns.

IRS: The federal agency tasked with enforcing tax laws and collecting taxes is the Internal Revenue Service (IRS). All businesses must maintain compliance with IRS regulations.

Liability: The term refers to the degree of personal risk and financial accountability for business debts and legal obligations.

Limited Liability Company (LLC): This business structure combines the liability protection of a corporation with the flexibility and tax benefits of a partnership.

Local Travel Expenses Deduction: You can deduct expenses incurred for business-related local travel, such as Uber or taxi fares.

Long-Term Capital Gains: These are profits from assets held for over a year that generally face reduced tax rates compared to short-term gains.

MACRS (Modified Accelerated Cost Recovery System): The United States primarily uses this depreciation method for federal income tax purposes.

Medicare Tax: A payroll tax supporting the Medicare program, which is also contributed to by employees and employers.

Mileage Rate: This rate determines the deduction you can claim for business-related mileage expenses when you use your vehicle for business purposes. It plays a crucial role in monitoring and recording your eligible transportation expenses.

Misclassification: Incorrectly categorizing workers as employees or independent contractors leads to legal and financial consequences.

Net Operating Loss (NOL): Business expenses exceed income, resulting in a loss. Understanding the rules for carrying forward or back NOLs is essential for tax optimization.

Office Supplies and Expenses Deduction: You can deduct expenses for everyday office supplies and larger purchases such as computers or smartphones for business purposes.

Partnership: This is a business arrangement where two or more individuals or entities work together, pooling their skills and resources to accomplish shared objectives.

Pass-Through Entity: In business structures such as partnerships or S corporations, income flows directly to the owner's tax return. Comprehending the mechanics of pass-through taxation is essential for effective tax planning.

Payroll Tax: Taxes deducted from employee salaries to fund social programs and services.

Professional Fees Deduction: You can deduct fees paid for services such as accounting or financial advising as essential business expenses.

Qualified Business Income Deduction (QBID): Small business owners can deduct a portion of their qualified business income, allowing them to optimize their tax savings. It's essential to assess your eligibility for this deduction.

Realized Gains: Profits that occur when you sell a capital asset.

Rent Deduction: The ability to fully deduct the cost of renting space for business operations, including office spaces and retail locations.

Rental Property Depreciation: The term refers to specific depreciation requirements for assets used in rental properties.
Research and Experimentation Tax Credit: A credit is available to businesses participating in research and

development activities.

Residential Clean Energy Credit: This refers to a tax credit for improving energy efficiency in residential properties.

Residual Value: The term refers to the asset's value after deducting depreciation.

S Corporation: A type of corporation that allows profits and losses to pass through to the owner's tax return, offering tax advantages while maintaining legal protections.

Sales Tax: Businesses collect customer taxes on eligible sales transactions, which vary based on the state and locality.

Salvage Value: The expected value of an asset that remains after its productive lifespan.

Section 125 Reporting: IRS regulations for pre-tax benefit plans and adjustable spending accounts.

Section 179 Deduction: A deduction that permits businesses to deduct the entire cost of eligible equipment in the year of its purchase, with a predetermined maximum limit.

Self-Employment Tax: Self-employed individuals pay taxes that encompass their contributions to Social Security and Medicare as employees and employers.

Short-Term Capital Gains: Short-term assets typically face higher profit tax rates when held for less than one year.

Small Business Health Care Tax Credit: Small businesses offering health insurance to their employees can take advantage of a tax credit.

Social Security Tax: Both employees and employers actively contribute to funding the Social Security program through payroll taxes.

Software Subscriptions Deduction: You can deduct expenses for essential business operations, such as point-of-sale software subscriptions.

Solar Investment Tax Credit (ITC): A tax credit for investments in solar energy projects, offering a 30% credit for projects starting construction before 2025.

Sole Proprietorship: This refers to a business arrangement where you, as the owner, hold complete control and take on personal responsibility for business debts and legal affairs.

Standard Deduction: As a small business owner, you need to understand the standard deduction, a predetermined dollar amount that reduces your taxable income and differs based on your filing status.

Start-Up and Organization Costs Deduction: Deduction for business starting costs, including licensing and permit fees.

State and Local Tax (SALT) Cap: The SALT cap limits the deduction of state and local taxes on federal tax returns, which can profoundly impact businesses in high-tax states.

Straight-Line Method: A depreciation method evenly allocates depreciation expenses throughout the asset's useful life.

A sum of the Years' Digits: Another accelerated depreciation method that spreads higher depreciation costs over an asset's useful life.

Tax Credits: Tax credits that reduce tax liability by an equal amount, such as the Child Tax Credit or American Opportunity Tax Credit.

Tax Cuts and Jobs Act: A significant tax reform law that changed various aspects of the tax code.

Tax Deductions: Deductible expenses are subtracted from income to calculate taxable income, encompassing deductions for business meals, travel expenditures, and costs related to a home office.

Tax Extension: A request for additional time to file a tax return, extending the deadline to evade late filing fines.

Tax Forms: To ensure accurate tax filing, it's crucial to understand which forms are necessary for your business structure when reporting income, deductions, and financial details to the IRS.

Tax Liability: Businesses and individuals are responsible for determining and paying the taxes they owe to the government. Effectively managing tax liability plays a crucial role in financial planning.

Tax Nexus: This describes the relationship between a business and a specific state, compelling the business to collect and remit sales tax within that state.

Tax Obligations: The legal requirements for reporting and paying taxes to government authorities, including income tax, sales tax, and payroll tax.

Tax Planning: Strategically overseeing your financial matters to reduce tax obligations while adhering to tax regulations is crucial for achieving financial success. Effective tax planning is a vital component of economic prosperity.

Tax Professional: A qualified expert who specializes in tax laws and can help you understand the tax implications of different business structures.

Tax Reform: Changes in tax laws and regulations enacted by the government. Staying informed about tax reform can help you adapt your tax strategies.

Tax Relief for American Families and Workers Act: Staying updated on legislative changes, including enhanced child tax credits and benefits for small businesses, is crucial to maximizing tax benefits.

Tax Return: A document submitted annually to the IRS that discloses income, deductions, and tax obligations.

Tax Withholding: Employers withhold income tax from an employee's paycheck, which depends on the employee's filing status and allowances.

Taxation: The taxation method applied to your business income varies based on the business structure, including pass-through and double taxation options.

Unrealized Gains: This term refers to the growth in the worth of an asset not yet realized as cash through a sale.

Useful Life: An asset's expected duration will be in use before it's considered fully depreciated.

Vehicle-Related Deductions: Expenses linked to business-operated vehicles, such as fuel, maintenance, and insurance, are eligible for deductions.

Volunteer Income Tax Assistance (VITA) Program: A program staffed by volunteers that offers free tax assistance to individuals with limited income.

W-2 Form: A form provided to employees annually summarizing their wages, withholdings, and other tax-related information.

Wash-Sale Rule: The IRS rule prohibits you from claiming a loss on a security if you purchase a substantially identical security within 30 days before or after selling it.

Work Opportunity Tax Credit (WOTC): Businesses receive a tax credit when they employ individuals from designated groups, such as veterans and the long-term unemployed.

Year-Round Tax Planning: The proactive approach of consistently managing and optimizing your business's tax obligations throughout the year to minimize liabilities and maximize tax benefits.

REFERENCES

Asmussen, B. (2023, December 5). *Small business laws and rules: The basics of payroll compliance.* CSI Blog. https://blog.csiaccounting.com/small-business-laws-rules-payroll-compliance

Berry-Johnson, J. (2023, December 27). *5 tax planning strategies for small businesses.* Lending Tree. https://www.lendingtree.com/business/year-end-tax-planning-strategies/

Business tax changes you need to know. (2023, January 2). Spiegler Blevins & Company. https://www.s-bcpas.com/resources/in-the-loop-magazine/2023-01-02/business-tax-changes-you-need-to-know

Capital gains tax on small business sale. (2023, October 16). Castro&Co. https://www.castroandco.com/blog/2023/october/capital-gains-tax-on-small-business-sale-castro-/

A costly situation for businesses: Section 174 capitalization is here. (2023, January 20). CLA. https://www.claconnect.com/en/resources/articles/2023/a-costly-situation-for-businesses-section-174-capitalization-is-here

The cost segregation depreciation guide for 2024. (n.d.). Specialty Tax Group. https://www.specialtytaxgroup.com/cost-segregation-depreciation-guide-for-2024

Deductions and credits for individuals and small businesses in tax

season 2024. (2023, October 16). Quantum Tax Consultants. https://quantumtax.com/blog/tax-deductions-credits-individuals-small-business-2024/

Depreciation changes for 2023. (2023, September 20). Intuit Accountants. https://accountants.intuit.com/taxpro center/tax-law-and-news/depreciation-changes-for-2023/

Donaldson, A. (2023, December 28). *5 ways new tax changes could affect small-business owners in 2024*. Inc. Magazine. https://www.inc.com/ali-donaldson/5-ways-taxes-could-affect-small-business-owners-in-2024.html

Emergency relief for small businesses under the CARES Act. (n.d.). Thomson Reuters. https://www.thomsonreuters.com/en/resources/covid-19-small-business-resources/emergency-relief.html

Fallon, D. (2023, October 17). *Employee benefits tax deductions: Guide for business owners*. U.S. chamber of commerce. https://www.uschamber.com/co/run/finance/employee-benefits-tax-deductions

Herigstad, S. (2023, October 24). *Small business taxes in 2024*. Business News Daily. https://www.businessnewsdaily.com/7720-small-business-taxes.html

How does the 2024 tax reform affect year-end tax planning for small businesses? (n.d.). Creative Advising. https://www.creative-advising.com/how-does-the-2024-tax-reform-affect-year-end-tax-planning-for-small-businesses/

How to categorize your business expenses. (2023, April 6). Square. https://squareup.com/us/en/the-bottom-line/managing-your-finances/how-to-categorize-business-expenses

How will potential changes in SALT affect tax planning for the 2024 tax year? (n.d.). Creative Advising. https://www.creative-advising.com/how-will-potential-changes-in-salt-affect-tax-planning-for-the-2024-tax-year/

Impacts of the 2023 bonus depreciation phase out. (2023, February 2). Lear & Pannepacker, LLP. https://lp-cpa.com/blog/2023-bonus-depreciation-phase-out/

Inflation Reduction Act energy tax credits. (2023, November 28). Bloomberg Tax. https://pro.bloombergtax.com/brief/business-energy-tax-credits/

Jafri, F. (2022, August 11). *10 best practices for small business record keeping.* Money. https://money.com/blog/small-business-record-keeping-best-practices

Johnson, J. A. (2023, February 22). *Your guide to 2023 tax credits.* Jeremy A. Johnson, CPA P.C. https://jajohnsoncpa.com/guide-to-tax-credits-for-small-businesses/

Lasker, R. (2022, August 5). *How to calculate federal unemployment tax (FUTA) in 2024.* The Motley Fool. Retrieved January 15, 2024, from https://www.fool.com/the-ascent/small-business/articles/futa/

Leonard, K. (2023, October 23). *COBRA insurance guide for small businesses.* Business News Daily. https://www.businessnewsdaily.com/15879-employers-guide-to-cobra.html

Lewis, S. S. (2023, January 13). *Small business tax planning | Top 10 strategies in 2024.* Lewis CPA. https://www.lewis.cpa/blog/small-business-tax-planning-top-strategies

Martinez, J. (2023, September 20). *51 accounting and

bookkeeping statistics for 2023. DocuClipper. https://www.docuclipper.com/blog/accounting-and-bookkeeping-statistics/

Maximize deductions: Smart tax strategies for small business owners in 2024. (n.d.). RinehimerBaker. https://rinehimerbaker.com/blog/maximize-deductions-smart-tax-strategies-for-small-business-owners-in-2024/

McIntyre, G. (2021, February 5). *21 small-business tax deductions you need to know.* NerdWallet. https://www.nerdwallet.com/article/small-business/small-business-tax-deductions-guide

Moran, N. (2022, December 1). *Small business taxes: 8 common questions answered ahead of tax season 2023.*

Exceptional Tax Services. https://www.exceptionaltaxservices.com/8-common-questions-answered-ahead-of-tax-season-2023/

New NFIB tax survey: High taxes remain a significant burden on small businesses. (2021, August 9).

The new tax laws and how they will affect small businesses. (2022, December 19).

The Blackwell Firm. https://theblackwellfirm.com/the-new-tax-laws-and-how-they-will-affect-small-businesses/

Niemann, P., & Lee, J. (2024, January 2). *2024 priorities for audit committees.* EY. https://www.ey.com/en_us/board-matters/priorities-for-audit-committees

Orem, T. (2023, November 9). *Tax credit vs. tax deduction.* NerdWallet. https://www.nerdwallet.com/article/taxes/tax-credit-vs-tax-deduction

Orem, T. (2024, January 2). *Capital gains tax: Meaning, rates, and calculator*. NerdWallet. https://www.nerdwallet.com/article/taxes/capital-gains-tax-rates

Parys, S., & Orem, T. (2024, January 8). *2024 tax filing guide: How to file taxes this year*. NerdWallet. https://www.nerdwallet.com/article/taxes/tax-filing

Pavilonis, K. (2023, November 30). *2023 year-end tax planning: What your business needs to know*. Cohen & Company. https://www.cohencpa.com/knowledge-center/insights/november-2023/2023-year-end-tax-planning-what-your-business-needs-to-know

Payroll tax compliance: Essential tips for small business owners. (n.d.). UZIO. https://www.uzio.com/resources/payroll-tax-compliance-essential-tips-for-small-business-owners/

Payroll taxes for small businesses. (2023, December 11). Block Advisors. https://www.blockadvisors.com/resource-center/small-business-services/payroll-tax/

Publication 946 (2022), How to depreciate property. (n.d.). IRS. https://www.irs.gov/publications/p946

Research & experimental expenses. (2023, January 25). PKF Mueller. https://www.pkfmueller.com/insights/tax/research-experimental-expenses

Rosenberg, E. (2023, May 31). *Working remotely tax implications*. Moneywise. https://moneywise.com/taxes/tax-implications
Sales tax 101 for online sellers. (2023, November 13). TurboTax. https://turbotax.intuit.com/tax-tips/self-employment-taxes/sales-tax-101-for-online-sellers/L4uTQCaIx

Sehmbi, K., & Kriss, R. (2023, May 11). *Small-business statistics: Numbers to know for 2023*. NerdWallet. https://www.nerdwallet.com/article/small-business/small-business-statistics

Shelton, C. (2023, November 29). *The small business's guide to straight line depreciation*. ChamberofCommerce.org. https://www.chamberofcommerce.org/small-businesss-guide-to-straight-line-depreciation

Small business health care tax credit and the SHOP marketplace. (2023, November 15). IRS. https://www.irs.gov/affordable-care-act/employers/small-business-health-care-tax-credit-and-the-shop-marketplace

Small business, innovation, and tax policy: A review. (n.d.). Brookings Institution. https://www.brookings.edu/articles/small-business-innovation-and-tax-policy-a-review/

Small business tax issues. (2021, March 24). Block Advisors. https://www.blockadvisors.com/resource-center/small-business-tax-prep/small-business-owner-unintended-tax-consequences/

Small business tax planning strategies for 2023. (2023, August 16). Accounting Insights from Borland Benefield. https://blog.borlandbenefield.com/small-business-tax-planning-strategies-for-2023/

Smiles, A. (2019, June 17). *7 commonly overlooked tax deductions for small businesses*. Gusto. https://gusto.com/resources/articles/taxes/overlooked-small-business-tax-deductions

Standberry, S. (n.d.). *34 big tax deductions (write-offs) for businesses in 2024*. My CPA Coach. https://mycpacoach.com/

blog/small-business-tax-deductions/

Straight-line depreciation explained. (n.d.). Xero. https://www.xero.com/us/guides/straight-line-depreciation-explained/

Tamplin, T. (2024, January 9). *Capital gains tax rate 2024 | Overview and calculation.* Finance Strategists. https://www.financestrategists.com/tax/tax-planning/capital-gains/capital-gains-tax-rate-2023/

Tax credits for accommodating disabled workers. (2023, April 13). TWHC. https://www.twhc.com/resources/blog/tax-credits-for-accommodating-disabled-workers/

Tax implications of different business structures. (2023, July 27). IFindTaxPro. https://ifindtaxpro.com/tax-blog/tax-implications-of-different-business-structures/

Tax planning for business owners and executives for 2024. (2023, December 20). Grant Thornton. https://www.grantthornton.com/insights/articles/tax/2023/tax-planning-for-business-owners-and-executives-for-2024

Tax tip 2023-66: Tax benefits to help offset the cost of making businesses accessible to people with disabilities. (n.d.). GovDelivery. https://content.govdelivery.com/accounts/USIRS/bulletins/359e896

Thomas-Bryant, K. (2018, July 6). *A taxing problem: The impact of tax on small businesses.* Sage. https://www.sage.com/en-gb/blog/a-taxing-problem/

3 tax changes for small businesses in 2024. (2024, January 2). Insight Law. https://www.insightlawfirm.com/blog/2024/01/3-tax-changes-for-small-businesses-in-2024/

The top 10 bookkeeping mistakes small businesses make. (2023, September 26). SCORE.org. https://www.score.org/resource/article/top-10-bookkeeping-mistakes-small-businesses

Topic no. 704, Depreciation. (n.d.). IRS. https://www.irs.gov/taxtopics/tc704

25 small business tax deductions to know in 2024. (2023, December 19).

FreshBooks. https://www.freshbooks.com/hub/expenses/tax-deductions-small-business

2024 business tax law: key compliance & strategy guide. (n.d.). GreenGrowth CPAs. https://greengrowthcpas.com/2024-business-tax-laws-mastering-compliance-strategy/

2024 business tax laws: Mastering compliance & strategy. (n.d.). GreenGrowth CPAs. https://greengrowthcpas.com/2024-business-tax-laws-mastering-compliance-strategy/

2024 federal payroll tax rates. (n.d.). Abacus Payroll Inc. https://abacuspay.com/resources/payroll-tax-wage-rates/2024-federal-payroll-tax-rates/

2024 tax law changes and updates to deduction limits. (n.d.). FlyFin. https://flyfin.tax/blog/tax-law-changes-for-2024-a-self-employed-guide

2023 capital gains rates. (n.d.). Bradford Tax Institute. https://bradfordtaxinstitute.com/Free_Resources/2023-Capital-Gains-Rates.aspx

2023 Small business statistics. (2023, March 17). Lendio. https://www.lendio.com/blog/small-business-statistics/

2023 year-end tax planning strategies for businesses. (2023, November 28). Cherry Bekaert. https://www.cbh.com/guide/

articles/2023-year-end-tax-planning-strategies-for-businesses-2/

The ultimate small business guide for tax season 2023. (2023, July 25). Fyle. https://www.fylehq.com/blog/tax-season

Understanding the tax relief for American families and workers act of 2024. (2024, January 22). Thomson Reuters. https://tax.thomsonreuters.com/blog/understanding-the-tax-relief-for-american-families-and-workers-act-of-2024/

Upcoming IRS improvements for small business owners. (2023, May 5). IRS. https://www.irs.gov/newsroom/upcoming-irs-improvements-for-small-business-owners

Verbeck, T. (2023, December 21). *Tax planning strategies for small business.* Nav. https://www.nav.com/business-taxes/tax-planning-strategies/

Waddell, M. (2024, January 16). *New tax bill includes 100% bonus depreciation.* ThinkAdvisor. https://www.thinkadvisor.com/2024/01/16/new-tax-bill-includes-100-bonus-depreciation/

Warshaw, J. (2024, January 5). *23 common tax deductions for small-business owners.* Ramsey Solutions. https://www.ramseysolutions.com/taxes/small-business-tax-deductions

Watson, J. (2023, November 3). *Value of a business tax deduction - Tax write-offs.* Watson CPA Group. https://wcginc.com/kb/value-of-a-business-tax-deduction/

What business owners need to know about filing taxes in 2024. (2024, January 10). CorpNet. https://www.corpnet.com/blog/business-owners-filing-taxes-in-2024/

What strategies can we use to minimize capital gains tax in 2024? (n.d.). Creative Advertising. https://www.creative-advising.com/what-strategies-can-we-use-to-minimize-capital-gains-tax-in-2024/

When to file. (n.d.). IRS. https://www.irs.gov/filing/individuals/when-to-file

Wiebe, J. (2023, April 30). *Full-time vs part-time employees: A guide for employers.* Gusto. https://gusto.com/resources/articles/hr/team-management/difference-part-time-full-time-employee

Wood, C. (2023, November 16). *Two IRS publications tout work opportunity tax credit.* Thomson Reuters tax and accounting. https://tax.thomsonreuters.com/news/two-irs-publications-tout-work-opportunity-tax-credit/

Work opportunity tax credit. (n.d.). IRS. https://www.irs.gov/businesses/small-businesses-self-employed/work-opportunity-tax-credit

Your checklist to prepare for IRS audits in 2023. (2023, March 4). Milikowsky Tax Law. https://www.caltaxadviser.com/your-checklist-to-prepare-for-irs-audits-in-2023